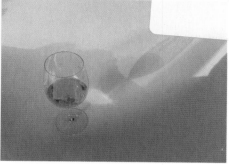

"Reflecting on a yellow floor"

Relaxing, peaceful with energy, like a meadow, the feeling is to be attracted outside.
And after a days work the voltage drops completely and puts you in a good mood.
It's not a strange thing, the yellow floor in a house.
It is just a matter of light.

Simone Turkewitsch, grandson of Livio Vacchini,
on Vacchini's Summer House where his parents live in Ticino, Switzerland.

The Constructed Floor
QUB MArch 2014

Editor
Colm Moore

Assistant Editors
Nadine Graham
Alice Nickell
Ryan O'Neill
Sean Sloan

Series Editors
Andrew Clancy and Colm Moore

Publisher
Queens Architectural Press
David Keir Building
Stranmillis Road
Belfast
BT9 5AG
United Kingdom

First Edition: 2014

Printed in Belfast
by Nicholson & Bass

ISBN 978-1-909731-02-8

Foot Size: 295 mm
Shoe Size EU: 44
Shoe Size UK: 9.5

Diagram Scale 1:50

Students

Andrew Abraham
Trudy Anderson
Ashlee Bell
Morgan Bernard
James Boyd
Finbar Bradley
Aaron Callen
Hua Kang Chin
Nathalie Claes
Tom Cosgrove
Sean Cullen
Rita Farrell
Ciara Geary
Stephanie Gibbons
Aine Grace
Nadine Graham
Sasha Greig
James Grieve
Andrew Hamon
Patrick Hoban
Justin Hughes
Erl Johnston
Patrick Jones
Conor Kerr
Mark Kiely
Magdalena Kisiel
Wouter Lenaerts
Romain Lossy
Matthew Macartney
Julian Manev
Orla McCann
Cormac McAteer
Ciara McCallion
James McCallister
Aoife McConaghy

Sinead McGahon
Barry McGowan
Eva McGowan
Aaron McGrady
Andrew McIlroy
Eoin McKenna
Michael McKeown
Lauren McLaughlin
Donal McMullan
Brian McQuillan
Patrick McShane
Ronnie Murray
Megan Nelson-Nilehn
Alice Nickell
Onila Nonis
Aodh O'Neill
Ryan O'Neill
Kyle Oliver
Declan Price
Fergal Rainey
Jill Richardson
Daniel Savage
Naomi Sheehan
Blaine Sherry
Ryan Simpson
Sean Sloan
Jason Stead
Antonis Stylianou
Gareth Taylor
Stuart Thompson
P.C. Wan
Christopher Watson
Megan White
Samuel Wigginton
Kaxi Zhang

Masters Coordinator

Gary Boyd - Reader

Module Coordinator

Andrew Clancy - Senior Lecturer

Tutors

Prof Michael McGarry - Head of
Architectural Design
Prof Greg Keefe - Director of
Research
Alan Jones - Senior Lecturer,
Director of Research
Colm Moore - Senior Lecturer
Ian McKnight - Senior Lecturer
John McLaughlin - Senior lecturer
Cian Deegan - University Tutor

Guest Critics

Rosamund Diamond - Honorary
Principal Lecturer UCL, Director
Diamond Architects
Maud Cotter - Artist
Sarah Sheridan - Dublin Institute of
Technology
Jude Barber - University of
Strathclyde, Director Collective
Architecture
Grainne Hassett - Senior Lecturer
SAUL, Director Hassett Ducatez
Architects
Sarah Lappin - Lecturer QUB

Contents

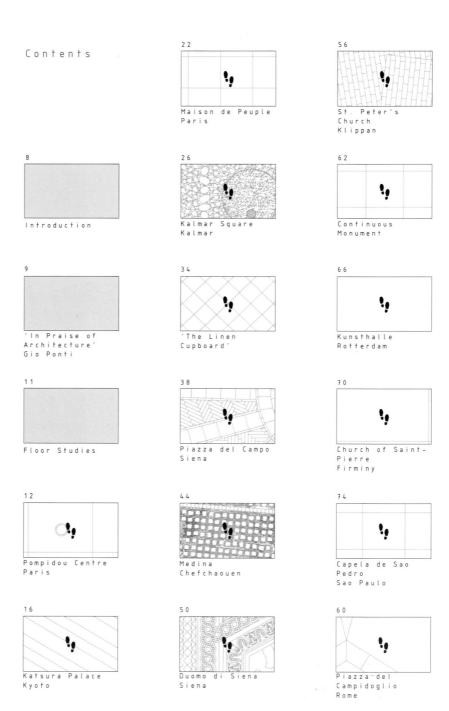

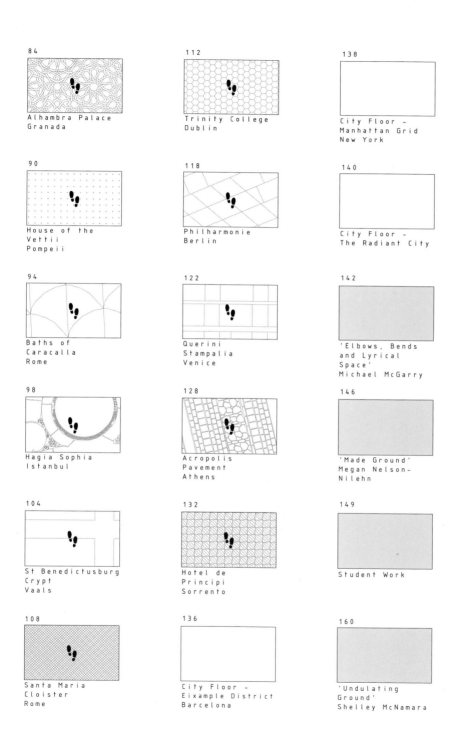

84
Alhambra Palace
Granada

112
Trinity College
Dublin

138
City Floor –
Manhattan Grid
New York

90
House of the
Vettii
Pompeii

118
Philharmonie
Berlin

140
City Floor –
The Radiant City

94
Baths of
Caracalla
Rome

122
Querini
Stampalia
Venice

142
'Elbows, Bends
and Lyrical
Space'
Michael McGarry

98
Hagia Sophia
Istanbul

128
Acropolis
Pavement
Athens

146
'Made Ground'
Megan Nelson-
Nilehn

104
St Benedictusburg
Crypt
Vaals

132
Hotel de
Principi
Sorrento

149
Student Work

108
Santa Maria
Cloister
Rome

136
City Floor –
Eixample District
Barcelona

160
'Undulating
Ground'
Shelley McNamara

Introduction

Colm Moore, Andrew Clancy
2014

As students we had the pleasure of Kenneth Frampton visiting our school on review day. He talked lyrically about the physicality of constructing space. Most strikingly that day he spoke about floors. He talked, as he wrote in his Studies on Tectonic Culture, about Alvar Aalto's Saynatsalo Town Hall. In particular he described the journey from entrance to council chamber. The brick stairs as an extrusion of the ground and the point of threshold to the civilized realm of council chamber emphasized by an arrival onto a suspended timber floor, highly polished and flexing under one's own weight. A well tempered environment, established decorum. Later the same day, he spoke of a film director whom when asked why he insisted the floor of the set be constructed with end grain timber blocks stated simply, because the end grain makes you stand up straight. The floor was charged, the room was electric.

Every building must start with an excavation of ground. We begin by cultivating a terrain, negotiating geology, typology, making a platform, defining a territory - a raft, a footing, a plinth, a floor. The enabling works. Fundamentally the floor is infrastructural, a foundation and surface to support the building and its life. And more, the floors delimits a territory, an interior prospect, for the eye and the body to explore. Its horizontal surface is gravitational and fluid providing resistance to the controlled falling of vaulting limbs. The floor traces the inevitable wear of the feet that strike it, bearing testament to occupation by mapping habit. It tempers both our environment and manner. Yet given its primary founding status as the point where the building becomes the ground the floor is overlooked, physically and literally. Before shelter, before enclosure, there is only ground. This semester our masters studio is firmly rooted to it.

'In the Praise of Architecture'

Gio Ponti
1960

The floor is a theorem. The Austrian Architect Strnad (or was it Franck?) has said, "Architecture is something finite in nature". It is also "something in-finite", besides being something unfinished and never finished (time has claims upon it and this means transformation). Architecture, like every work of art is unchangeable, eternal in a single form; it is an ordering of the disorder of nature. But nature is neither disorder nor order; it is a harmony.

Architecture establishes a different kind of harmony in the "natural" harmony of nature; it is a harmony that acts in contrast, a harmony of geometry (etymologically speaking this word does not adhere to its literal meaning any more; geometry is not at all geo-metric, earth measuring; it is abstract and mathematical and therefore free from geo). This architectonic order interposed in nature begins with a floor. The floor is a theorem, the projection of the crystal, the checkerboard on which play all the mobile and living elements (including man) that integrate architecture and live in it.

The floor is, and must be a game of materials. It must establish sequences of materials as well as colours, dimensions and forms. To go over it must be an adventure (and more than a pedestrian one). The floor – a fantastic and precise finitude, a progression or succession prescribing its own limit. The floor, if architecture is to live by all its resources must not be effective on only one level. It must have three dimensions, that is, it must represent a play of levels. Remember that.

Just as the proof of a theorem can be reversed from the QED to the proposition, and just as addition is the proof of subtraction, so one must be able to turn back on a floor and retrace ones steps. This reversed sequence is the test of the floor, the test to prove it is right. (Walls merge into polished floors, the polished floor is a lake. We fly over it; otherwise we fall. It is made for dancing. We cannot sleep in a room with a polished floor.) Because we walk on the floor, our movement moves from off the floor, which is the canto fermo of motion. Our movement creates spectacles, the initial spectacles of architecture.

A spectacle is watched by staying still; the spectator is still, and the show moves in front of their eyes with its parade of emotions. Music is heard by staying still (when one is not dancing; when dancing, one listens to two things), and the music develops inside us (or in front of us, who knows?). Architecture on the other hand stands still, and its spectator moves. When architecture is really beautiful, it unfolds along the steps and the glances of the spectator in a sequence of surprises, drops, crescendos, finales.

Do you understand me? It is a show that is produced by its being passed through – by passing through it in every direction, coming and going, and looking around, looking up. The architect must be the director of this difficult and total performance. Think about this, and you will see how one can notice immediately – by going through it without emotions – just what poor, tired, lazy sleepy architecture actually is (I mean the architecture of poor, tired, lazy, sleepy architects).

The other kind, true architecture, the kind that sings, that plays, takes us into its spaces and makes us walk in them, go back and forth in them; it makes our hearts beat faster from room to room, from diversity to diversity, from play of fancy to play of fancy, from light to light.

Architecture is peripatetic. It is music and our spirit dances to its tune. It must move us with its sequences, invite us to go beyond every threshold, to run up every stair, to lean like a child from every window, to peer down every one of its flights of perspective. It must make us nostalgic for what we have seen, make us want to retrace our steps, fall in love with its sights, remember them always. We must pursue this invisible director – the architect (how I wish I could say well what I wish to say!)

Floor Studies

Centre Pompidou, Paris
Richard Rodgers & Peter Rice

Trudy Anderson
Tom Cosgrove

The Pompidou Centre in Paris is perhaps the definitive
model for hi-tech architecture. The centre comprises a
variety of functions, hosting a public library, museum of
modern art, acoustic research centre, and a large section of
administrative accommodation. The architects, in conjunction
with Irish engineer Peter Rice, exploited the infrastructure
of the building and literally turned it inside out. To define
a clear expression of purpose and accommodate a diverse
range of activities within the building, mechanical and
structural systems are shifted to the external facades.
Hence, the floor, which would routinely be interrupted by
columns, stairs, lifts and ducts, is free and unbroken. The
steel grid structure allows reinforced concrete floor slabs
to be inserted, dismantled and reconfigured as necessary,
providing a perfect setting for large exhibitions and
displays. Notably, this cultural centre, accessible at street
level, also extends it's municipal space out into the city.
The building itself occupies just half of the overall site,
donating the remaining ground of generous civic proportions
as a piazza for the citizens of Paris.

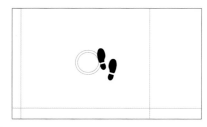

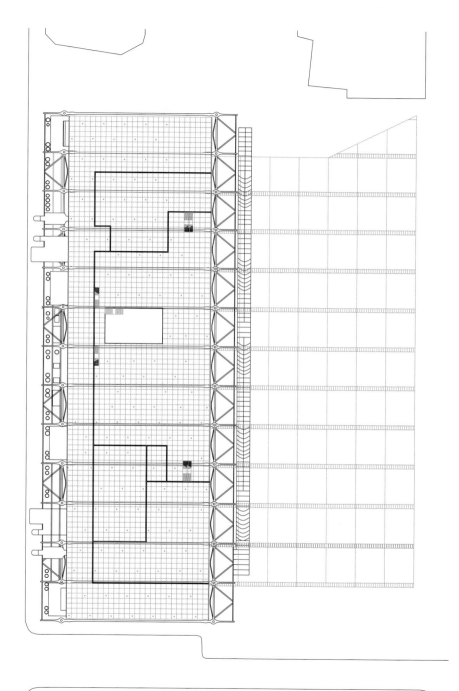

5m

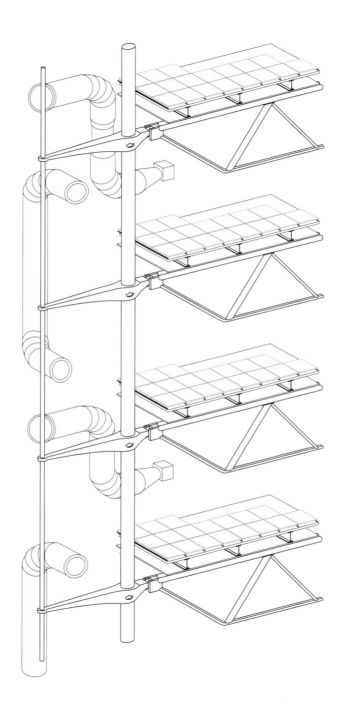

1m

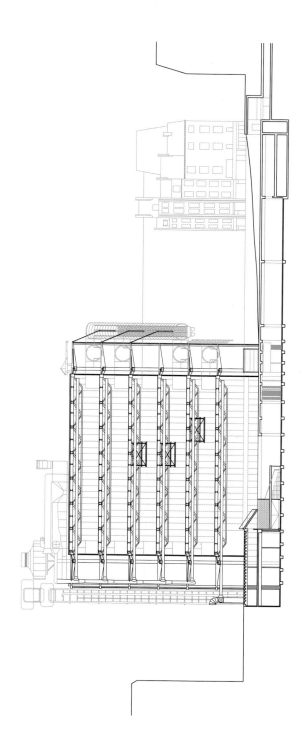

]5m

Katsura Imperial Palace, Kyoto
Kobori Enshu

Aoife McConaghy
Aodh O'Neill

Katsura Imperial Villa was built by Kobori Enshu in the wooded suburbs of Kyoto and is renowned as one of the finest examples of traditional Japanese architecture. The villa comprises of the 'Old Shoin', the 'Middle Shoin' and the 'New Palace' along with elaborately detailed gardens and Tea Houses. The simple post and beam structure and lightweight partitions of the villa create a flexible interior space. The structure is elevated from the ground and utilises traditional, multifunctional Tatami mats as an extended floor covering. These Tatami mats, made from rice and straw with cloth edging, measure exactly twice as long as they are wide, at a ratio of 2:1. Laid on the ground, their dimensions determine floor area, room size and partitions, and are seen to set up harmonious interior spaces. Decorative and lightweight wall partitions allow light to diffuse into the rooms of the villa, over this most tactile and prescriptive of floor surfaces.

5m

10m

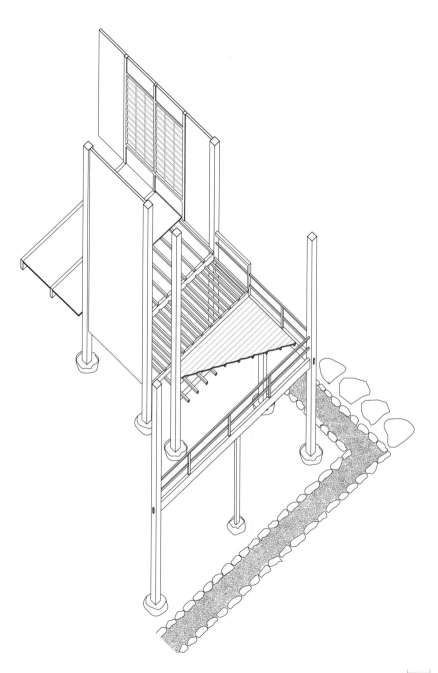

0.5m

La Maison du Peuple, Clichy
Jean Prouve

Patrick McShane
Christopher Watson

The Maison de Peuple was constructed between 1935 and
1938 and was designed by a team of architects including
Jean Prouve and Vladimir Bodiansky. The maison is
located in Clichy, a town on the outskirts of Paris and
was commissioned by it's mayor, who was keen to improve
existing market facilities and provide accommodation for
culture and leisure activities. In order to accommodate a
variety of functions, the architects designed a number of
adaptable spaces and innovative technical solutions allowing
them to function. Walls throughout the complex are non-
loadbearing and instead suspended from the structure
itself. The ground throughout the Maison de Peuple is
particularly ingenious. Floor slabs on the first level are
removable and can be stacked to allow a void onto the
market on the floor below. In addition, the glass roof is
retractable to allow light and air into the building for
comfort and recreation. Versatility of these spaces through
mechanisms of the floor demonstrates a sophisticated
interpretation to the notion of beauty and function.

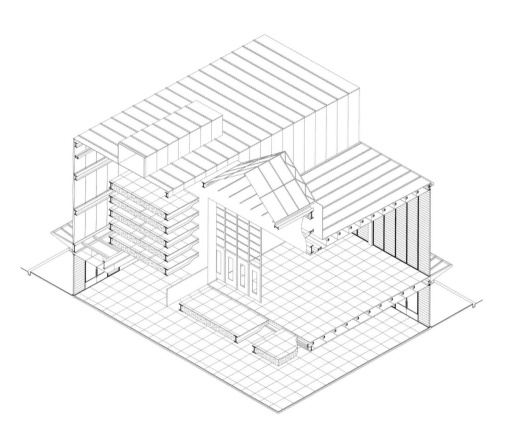

1m

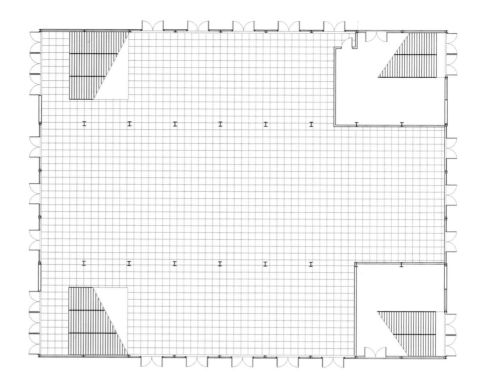

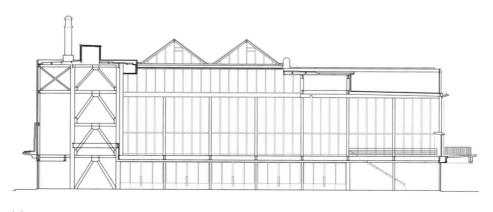

1m

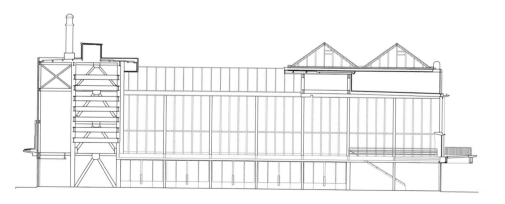

Kalmar Square
Caruso St John

Daniel Savage
Gareth Taylor

The principal public square in Kalmar, which boasts a 300
year history, was renewed in 2003 by Caruso St John
Architects and artist Eva Lofdahl in order to accommodate
evolving functions and to redefine the public square as a
contemporary place in the city. Tactile surfaces across the
floor are employed to increase one's sensitivity towards the
significance of this public urban place. Pedestrian passages
and spaces for public gathering are defined by smooth
surfaces of precast concrete slabs and cut granite sets.
These zones are complimented by alternating areas of granite
field stones, pertaining to the original stones that were
first used to lay the floor of this public square. A number of
water chambers are set into the ground across the square,
fitted with a barred concrete lid. Passers-by may walk along
and hear the movement of water below, relating back to the
city's historic wells. Resting on top of the textured ground
surface are a number of artistic intervention lighting masts.

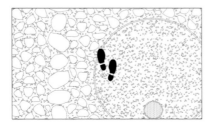

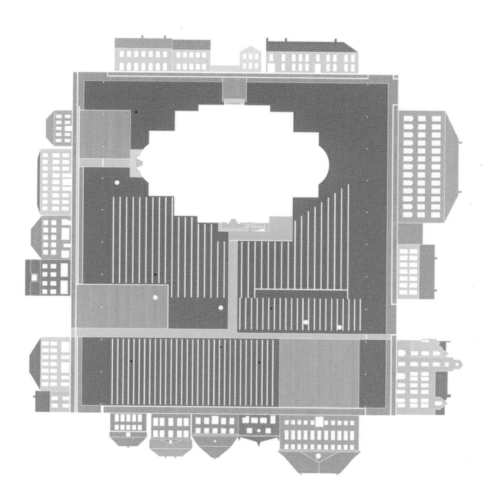

10m

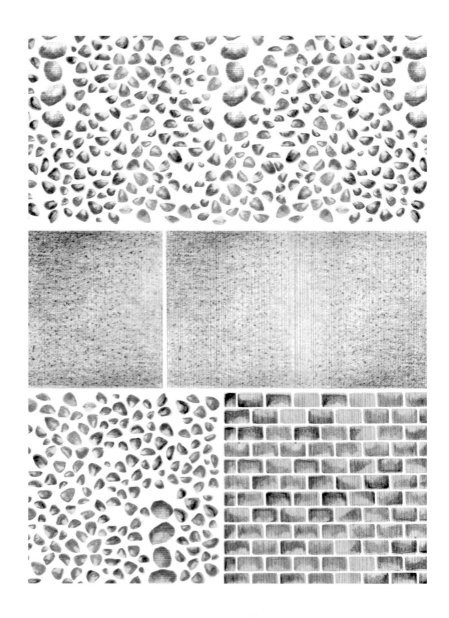

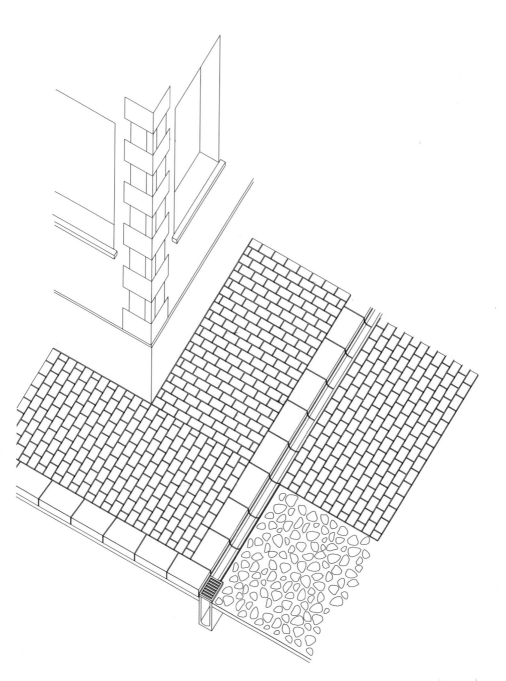

0 . 5 m

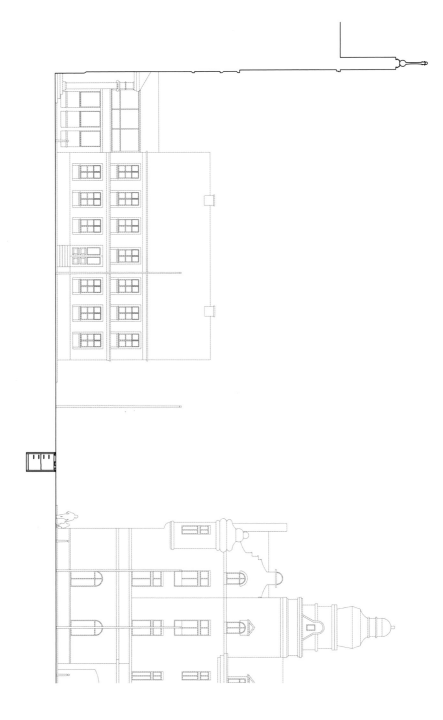

1m

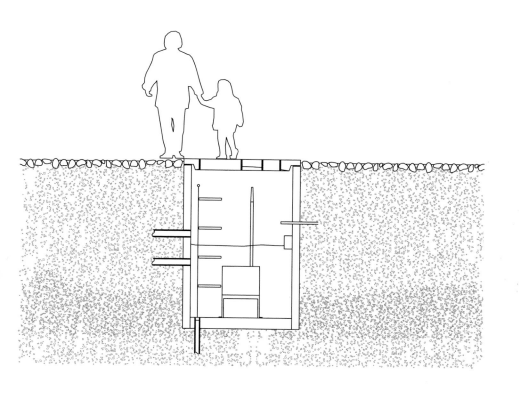

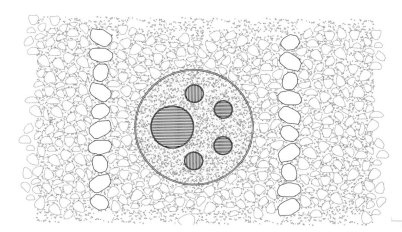

0 . 5 m

The Linen Closet, Amsterdam
Pieter de Hooch

Aine Grace
Sean Sloan

The concept of the floor goes much deeper than a surface by which to move around. A study of Pieter de Hooch's approach to his 1663 painting of the floor in 'The Linen Cupboard' demonstrates it's power to define the boundaries of a space, a street or a city. De Hooch, one of the masters of the Dutch Golden Age was famed for depicting domestic scenes, often with a series of views through to other spaces beyond the principal subject of the painting. In 'The Linen Cupboard', a rich palette of texture, colour, light and shade across the floor surfaces illustrate an architectural depth to the scene, unique to the city of Amsterdam. Beyond the principal room, a change in ground surface pertains to an alternative space, perhaps a kitchen or scullery. Though an open door, ground is substituted for the flowing water of one of Amsterdam's waterways, with a quaint cobbled path on the other side of this typically Dutch canal street. Throughout the depth of this scene, the floor exists as a distinct threshold between individual and inhabitant, public and private, street and home.

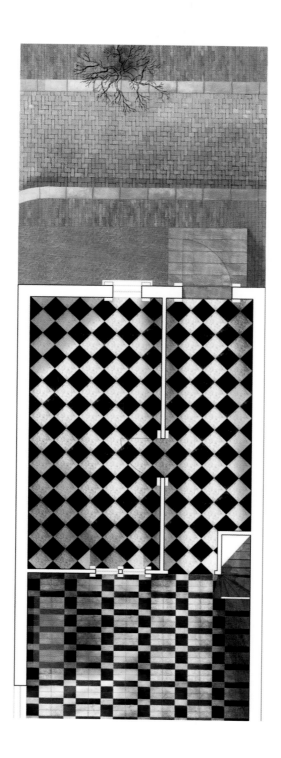

0.5m

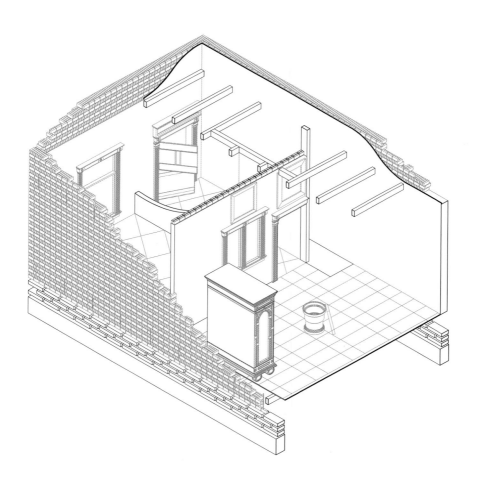

0.5m

Piazza del Campo
Various

Nadine Graham
James Grieve

Piazza del Campo hosts the principal public gathering place
in Siena, and provides a striking counterpoint to the city's
dense medieval streets beyond. Taking its form from the
underlying topography of the hillside, the floor slopes
gently from it's curved edges downwards toward the central
water drain and draws focus to the town hall overlooking
the piazza. This resultant concave and shell-like profile
sets up a quintessential venue for observing city life. The
piazza is defined by zones set out by herringbone brick
and stone paving, and affords Siena's citizens the choice
to promenade around the more formal edges, or to interact
with the central segments which are more suited to sitting
and play. The spoke-like paving radiating from the centre
of the piazza was commissioned in 1349 by Siena's ruling
body, the Council of Nine, to symbolise both their power
and the nine folds of the Madonna's cloak. Twice a year,
the city celebrates the Palio di Siena, where selected
riders from each ward race horses around the piazza
for the honour of their district. The floor in this event
plays an important role, with Siena's citizens gathering
according to their district in each of the nine triangular
brick segments in support of their chosen elective.

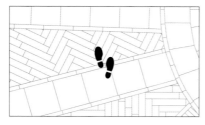

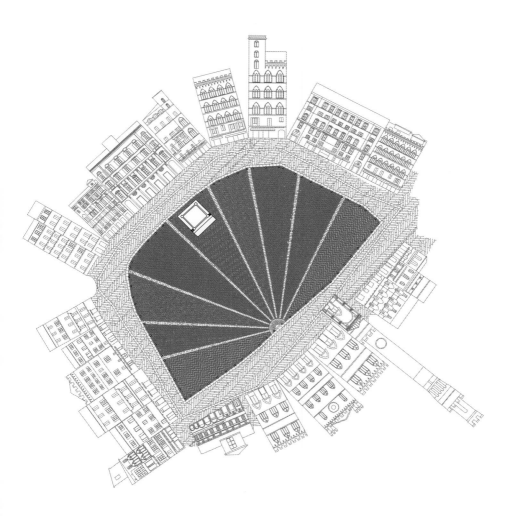

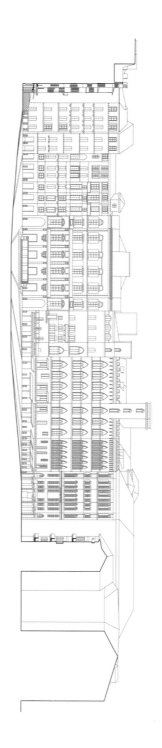

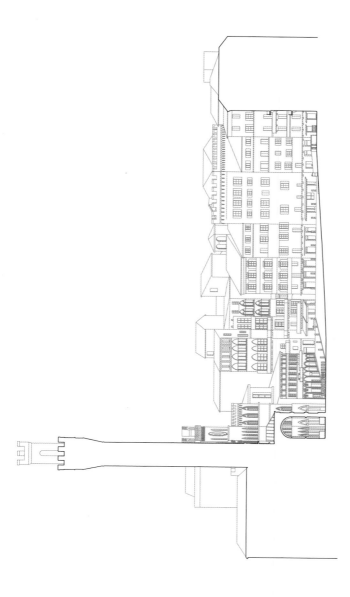

10 m

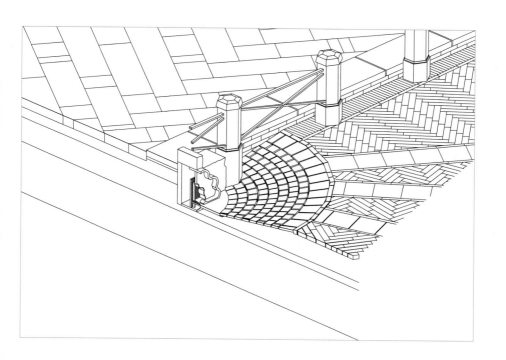

0.5m

Chefchouen, Morocco
Unknown

Megan White
Onila Nonis
Antonis Stylianou

The city of Chefchaouen is located between two peaks of
the Rif mountains in north west Morocco. Passing through
the medina of Chefchaouen one enters a labyrinth of bright
shades of blue, where houses, doors, stairs and passages are
painted in tones ranging from aquamarine to cobalt. A coded
network of streets is defined by a spectrum of blues, where
the public realm is pale, and more vivid shades are reserved
for private zones. The blue tones painted onto the stone
streets continue across the ground and extend up the edges
of properties, blurring the boundary between floor and walls.

Deep in the dense network of the medina, quiet residential
streets are painted a vibrant shade of blue, marking their
domain as private. Contrastingly, in places of heavy public
passage the blue paint and stones are worn bare, and
so here the tones are more muted, defining the place as
public realm. Although the Spanish Jewish community who
originally painted the streets blue as a reflection of their
faith in God have long since left the city, the tradition
of annually repainting Chefchaouen is maintained by it's
citizens, since this treatment of the floor has set up a
social framework by which people continue to use the city.

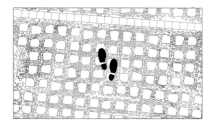

1m

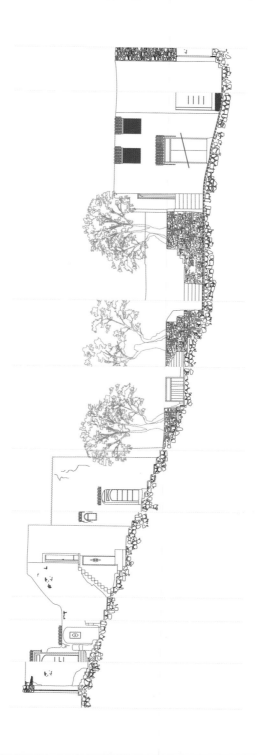

1m

1m

Duomo, Sienna, Italy
Giovvanni di Agostino

Ryan O'Neill
Donal McMullan
Romain Lossy

The pavement of the 'Duomo' effectively begins in the city, outside the cathedral, as the entrance steps rise from the piazza to form a hilltop podium amidst the narrow and winding cobbled streets of medieval Siena. Work on the cathedral began in 1369 and was edited over many years by more than forty artists, with a substantial restoration taking place in the late 19th century. The ornate workmanship of the floor evolved over time as artists adopted subtly different methods. The earliest and simplest 'graffito' method used large pieces of white marble which were shaped and assembled to form a silhouette, with details defined by engraving, piercing and and filling cavities with stucco. To accentuate the character of these rich materials, pieces of white marble make up the 'figure' and are inlaid with darker marble pieces which form the 'ground' portion of the images. The floor of the cathedral boasts 56 panels of elaborate marble mosaics, each representing scenes from the Old Testament. The rigorous use of contrasting tones across the floor surface heighten the striking internal atmosphere of one of Italy's most significant religious structures.

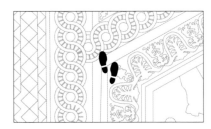

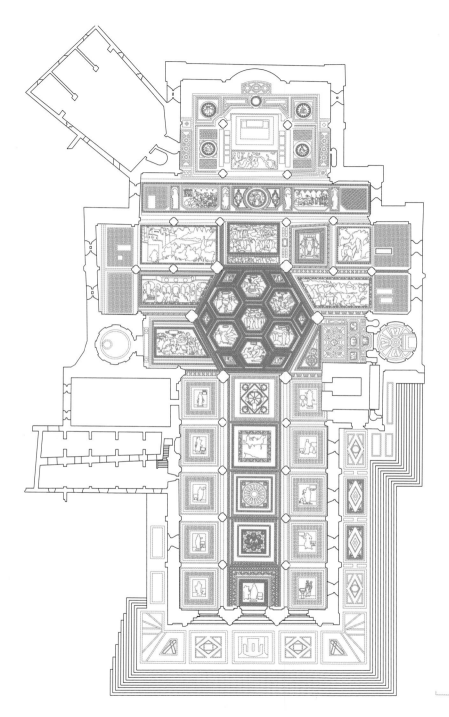

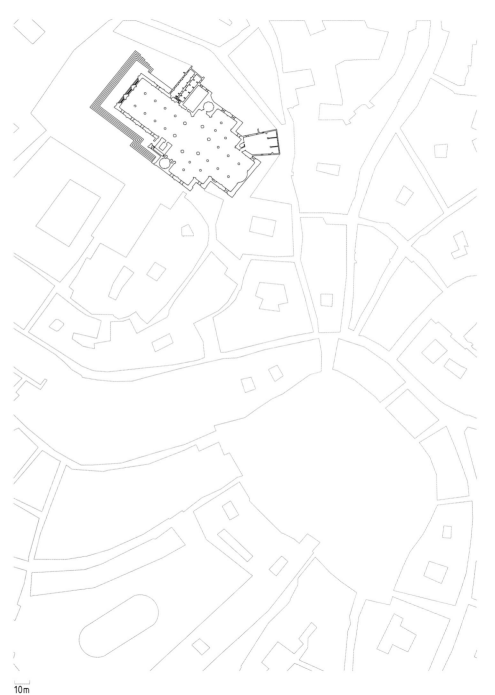

10m

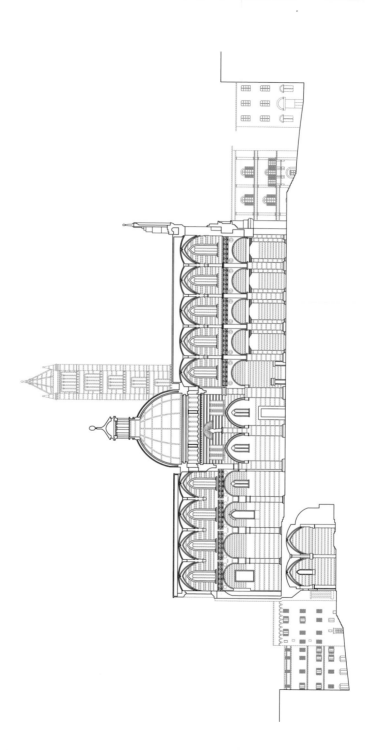

5m

One of the first mosaics to be laid, 'The Sienese She-Wolf Surrounded by the Emblems of Allied Cities'(1373). The She- Wolf and the suckling twins, around which lie the badges of the confederate cities, including Pisa, Lucca, Roma and Arezzo.

1m

Saint Peters, Klippan
Sigurd Lewerentz

Conor Kerr
Lauren McLaughlin

Rough dark brick is used ubiquitously throughout St Peter's church. Lewerentz imposed an unorthodox rule that a brick should never be cut, resulting in enormous joints achieved only by bulking out mortar with ground slate to make it act more like concrete. Within the church, brick forms the walls, the vaulted roof, the altar and pulpit, and of course the floor. The effect is dark, hard and rustic. It defines a space almost invisible until one's eyes adapt to the dimness. The brick is interrupted only by the baptismal channel at the corner where one enters. This delicate and instinctive tear in the floor, a water filled fracture, swells significantly at the edges, heightening the tension in this fragile atmosphere. The church is cave-like and intimate, more of a sanctuary of reflection than celebration, a space of deep mystery rather than explicit transparency.

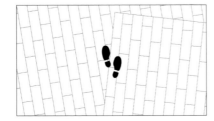

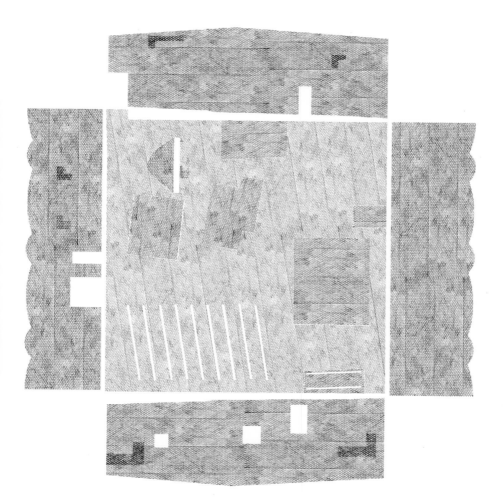

1m

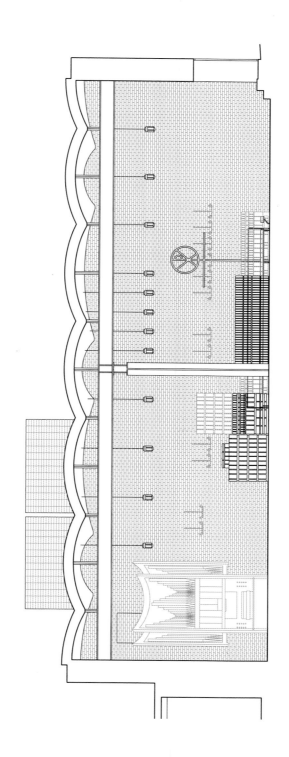

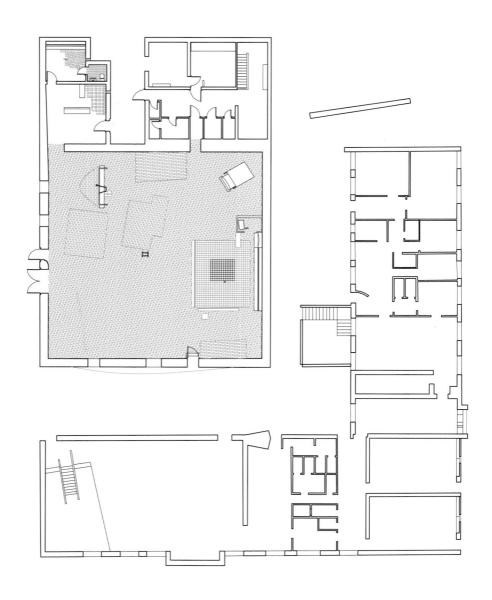

1m

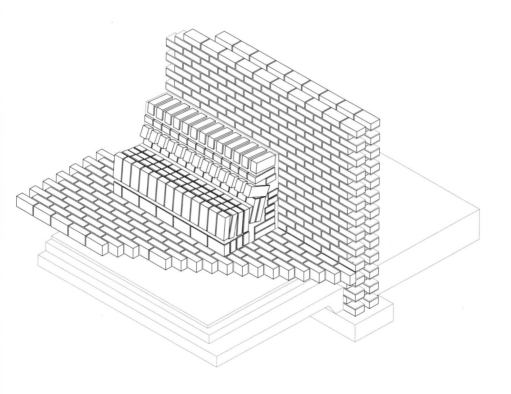

1m

Continuous Monument
Superstudio

Barney McQuillan
Patrick Hoban

The concept of the 'Continuous Monument' evolved
in 1969 among a group of Italian architects in Florence
who came to be known as the Superstudio collective.
Continuous Monument was the radical notion for a grid
megastructure to spread across the surface of the earth,
over land and seas, eventually enveloping the whole
planet. This sensational concept derived from a criticism
of consumerist culture and globalisation. The architects
made a playful attack on the International Style, lambasting
its blanket use of steel and concrete in architecture and
infrastructure across contemporary and historic cities,
regardless of tradition and culture. These exaggerated
comments on the loss of cultural identity and regionalism
were manifest in a series of striking images, known as
'Negative Utopias'. The architects created clever photo-
montages illustrating landscapes and cities being overtaken
by this white grid surface, both featureless and uniform.
These representations acted as a witty yet telling
metaphor, and remain relevant and powerful even today.

Introducing the continuous monument to Belfast.

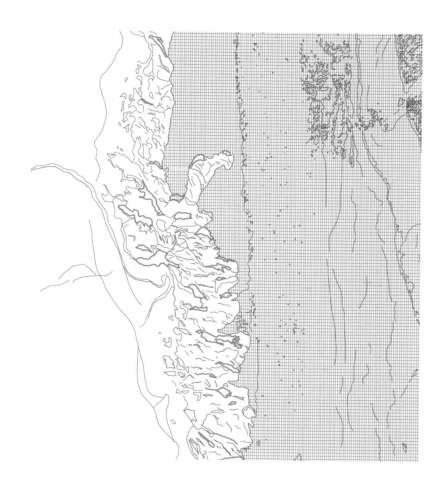

Kunsthalle, Rotterdam
Rem Koolhaas

P.C. Wan
Cormac McAteer
Jason Stead

The Kunsthal art museum is located in Rotterdam within the city's Museumpark complex and acts as an exhibition space for a range of temporary exhibitions and installations. The building and its pedestrian ramp serve to moderate the blunt transition between elaborate infrastructure of the expressway and the city parkland on opposing sides. The museum is a compilation of autonomous galleries and halls designed to offer utmost flexibility for touring exhibits and shows. Hence, the floor in this programme acts as a unifying element, a consistent concrete ramp which circulates around the halls inferring a degree of wholeness to this diverse collection of spaces and exhibits.

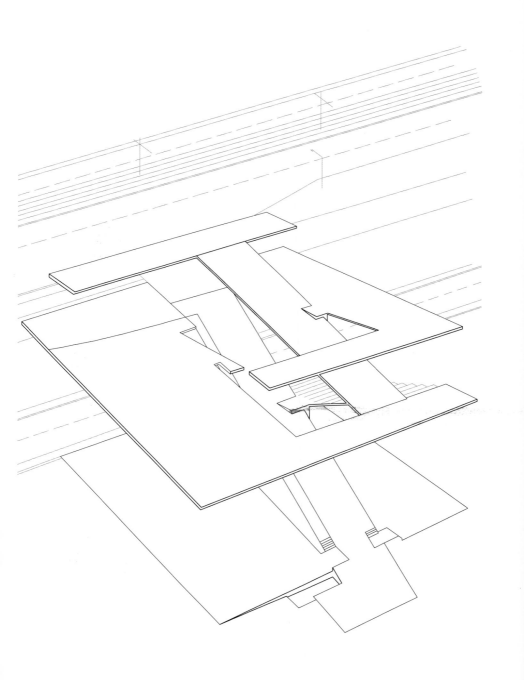

1m

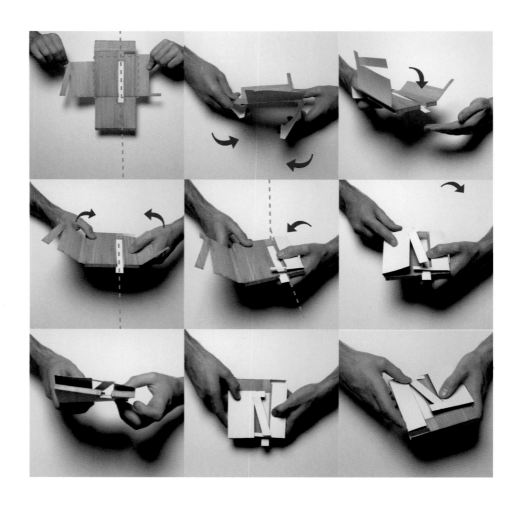

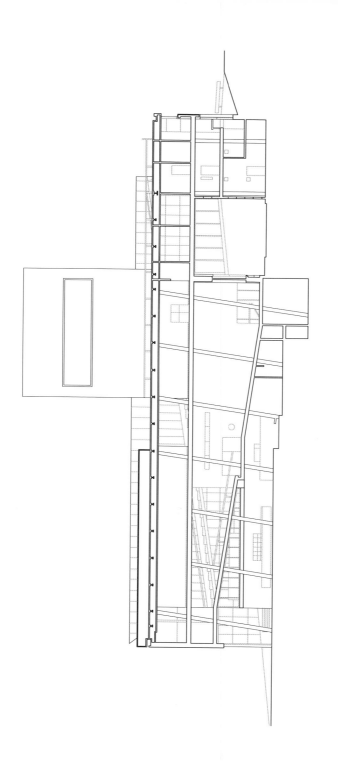

Saint-Pierre Church, Firminy
Le Corbusier

Orla McCann
Eoin McKenna

The Church of Saint Pierre in Firminy was the last project
of Le Corbusier, and was completed in 2006, long after
his death and under the guidance of his student, Jose
Oubrerie. Le Corbusier used the design of the church as
an opportunity to control light through extensive use
of concrete as a building material. Polished concrete
with visible pour lines flows across the ground floor
and extends upwards via an external ramp towards the
upper level. This uniform ground surface accentuates
the light and colours cast into the space by a series of
'light cone' apertures in the ceiling of the church. Colours
and pools of light are reflected by the polished concrete
floor and slowly creep across it as the day progresses.

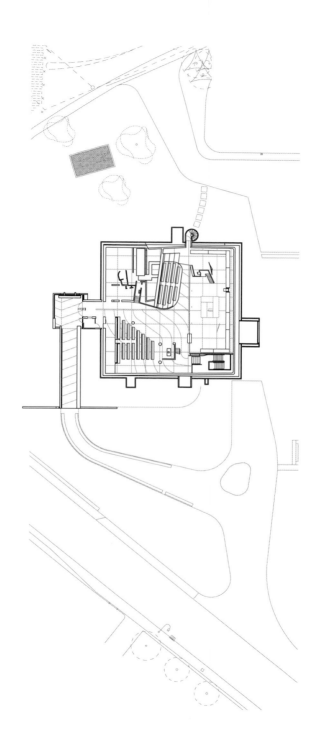

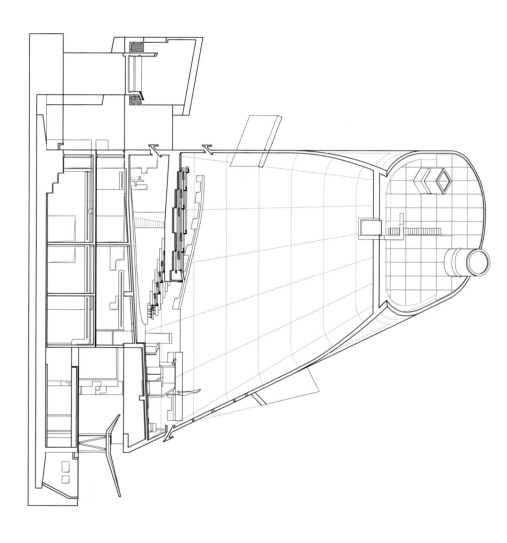

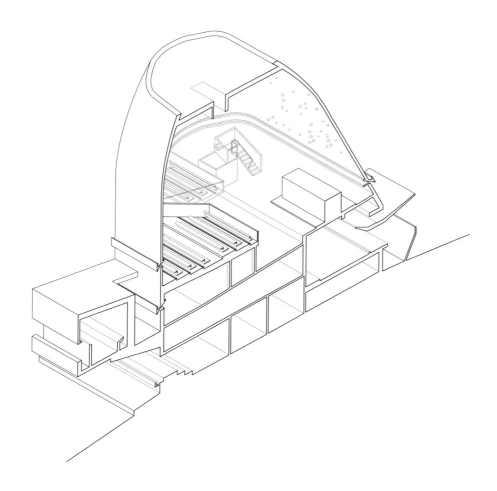

1m

Capela de Sao Pedro, Portugal
Paolo Mendes da Rocha

Michael McKeown
Fergal Rainey

Constructed in 1987, the innovative modernist Church of Saint Peter located near the Boa Vista Palace was constructed using a limited palette of concrete and glass. A two story glass façade looks over the Mantiquera Mountains. Religious spaces flow around a single 3.3m diameter column at the centre. The column allows the cantilevered curved first floor to appear as if it is floating above a pool of water below, creating a sense of strength and stability. This first floor, curved in both plan and section, appears as a solid heavy mass of concrete, but in reality cantilevered concrete fins are hidden beneath a concrete slab finish providing the structural stability needed to create the floating illusion. This illusion is emphasised further by the reflecting pool of water below. The roof is of similar construction, and is again supported by the column with structural concrete fins providing additional stability.

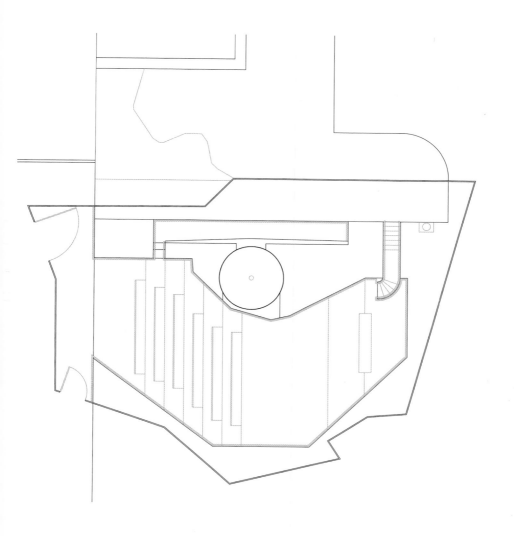

1m

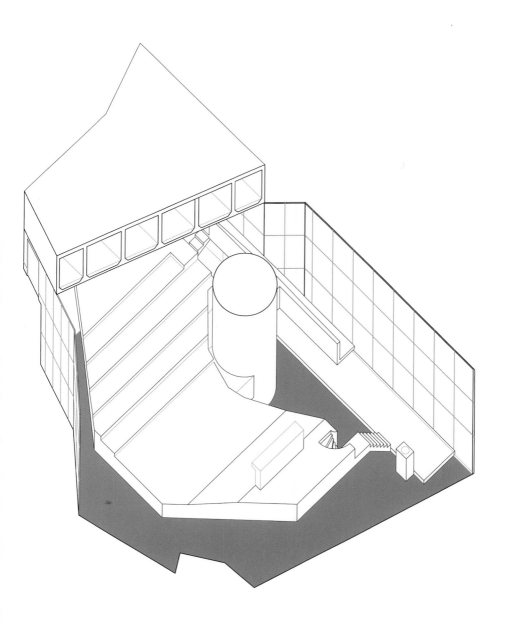

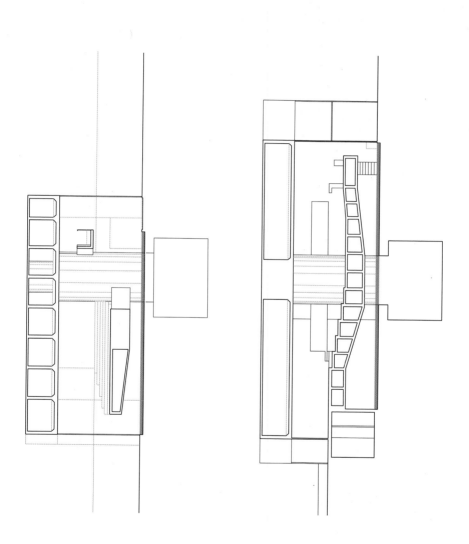

Piazza de Campodoglio, Rome
Michelangelo

Jill Richardson
Ryan Simpson

Commissioned by Pope Paul III and designed by Michelangelo in 1536, the Piazza del Campidoglio sits atop the Capitoline Hill as a symbol of Renaissance Rome. The piazza is trapezoidal in shape, surrounded by palazzos along the three principal sides. People arrive into this, the city's main civic space, by leisurely ascending the generous, ramped stair known as the Cordonata. Skirting the perimeter of the piazza, low steps rise towards the palazzos, and disappear into the paving as required by the subtle slope of the floor. At it's centre, the piazza hosts a slightly mounded oval profile, upon which sits the statue of Marcus Aurelius as the focal point of the space. The entire piazza is governed by axiality and symmetry, most noticeably across it's floor, with travertine paving setting up a complex geometric design relating to cosmological schemes. From every position, the curvilinear pathways outlined on the floor, combined with the implementation of the central statue, distract the eye from a single line of vision and create a sense of space in this outdoor room in the city.

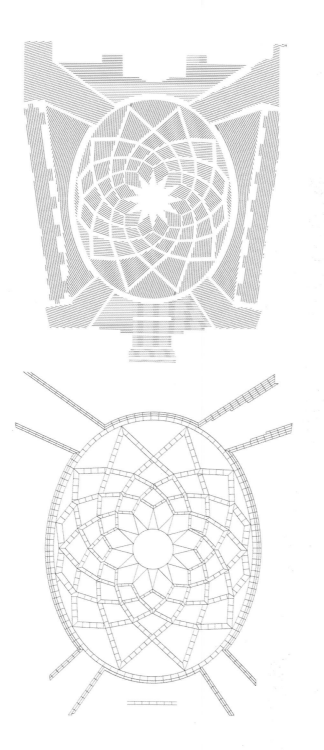

10m

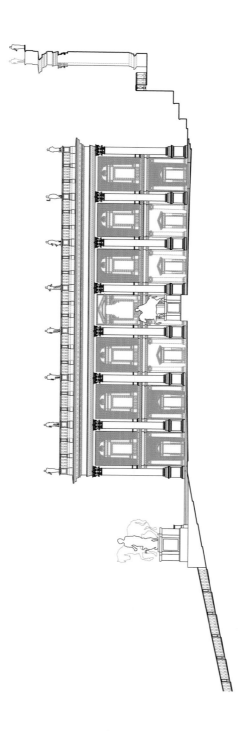

Alhambra, Granada
Various

James Boyd
Andrew Abraham
Morgan Bernard

Built by the last Muslims to rule Spain, the Nasrid dynasty, the Alhambra palace sits within walled confines atop its hillside as a sophisticated complex of palace, court and garden. The palace was designed for three distinct purposes – a home for the Nasrid ruler, a barracks for his military, and a medina for court officials. All sections of the complex are connected by an intricate network of paths, gardens and gateways. Across the confines of this walled city, threshold between interior and exterior, palace and garden, private and public is defined by the nature of the floor. Radical transition from cool and shaded palace suite to hot and exposed garden is moderated throughout by a series of arcaded patios. Solid walls give way to elaborately carved arches and columns, which are succeeded by plants and slender trees. Hence, the floor exists across the complex as an unambiguous threshold between spaces. Inside, surfaces comprise of geometric brick patterns interspersed with ceramic detailing. Beyond, shaded colonnades are laid with slabs of white marble before a delicate step down onto gravel courtyard. In addition to progression of surfaces, water is a key element in the Alhambra complex. It serves it's function for citizens of the medina and hydrates the abundant gardens and plants, while also appearing as a series of ornamental drains and pools set into the ground to cool and calm palace occupants.

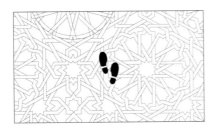

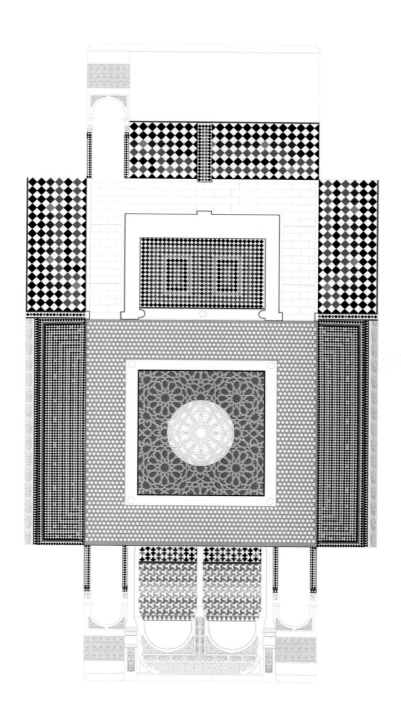

1m

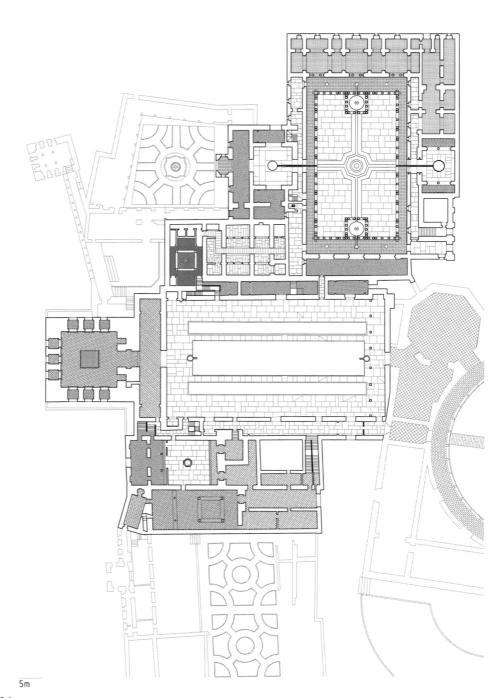

5m

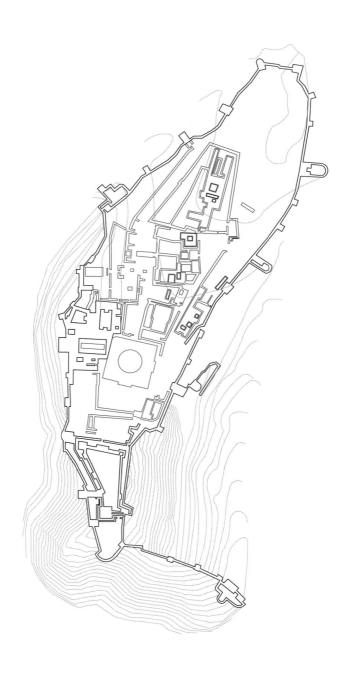

5m

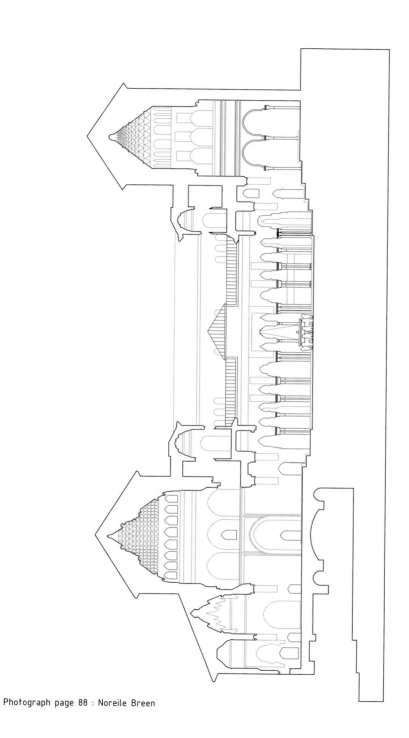

Photograph page 88 : Noreile Breen

1m

Casa dei Vettii, Pompeii
Unknown

Eva McGowan
Sam Wigginton

The Casa dei Vettii, built in the north-west of Roman
Pompeii, was home to two wealthy freemen, Aulus Vettius
Restitutus and Aulus Vettius Conviva. The house provides
an exemplary impression of a Roman town house, and was
built in the last of Pompeii's architectural styles, boasting
some of the finest preserved frescoes in this city of ruins.
The entrance to the house opens from a quiet street into
a Tuscan atrium. A compluvium in the roof corresponds with
a marble impluvium laid into the floor which collects falling
rainwater. This impluvium rests into the ground, as if it is a
solid object set into the earth-coloured floor. Surrounding
the impluvium is a pattern of white stones pressed into the
ground, known as 'opus signinum', setting up a rhythm to
the floor which extends throughout the house.

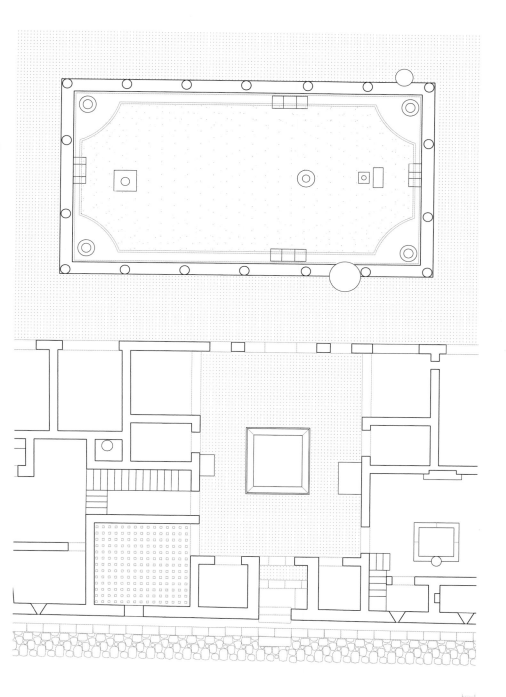

1m

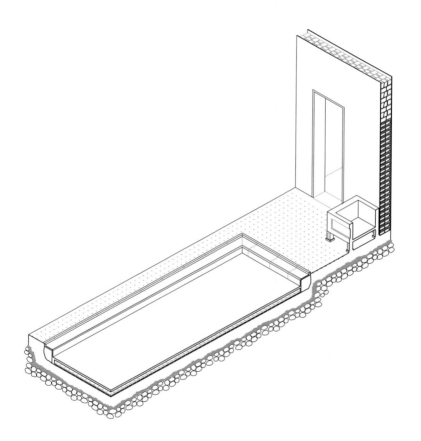

Baths of Caracalla, Rome
Septimius Severus

Barry McGowan
Ciara Geary
Matthew Macartney

The Baths provided one of the principal public bathing places, or 'thermae' in the city of Rome during the reign of Emporer Caracalla around AD 212. The floors of the baths demonstrate a prime example of both beauty and function. Decorative mosaics depicting mythical sea creatures and famous athletes of the era could be seen throughout the building above ground, to be enjoyed by the public using the baths. Below this decorative surface lay the hypocaust – the sophisticated Roman system of underfloor heating by means of burning coal and timber. The water which was heated was then transported throughout the building by aqueducts serving the baths.

The floor functions as a threshold between two worlds; the Roman citizens bathing in lavish surroundings above ground, and the hundreds of labourers maintaining the baths below in the gloomy underworld of subterranean vaults.

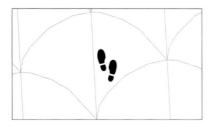

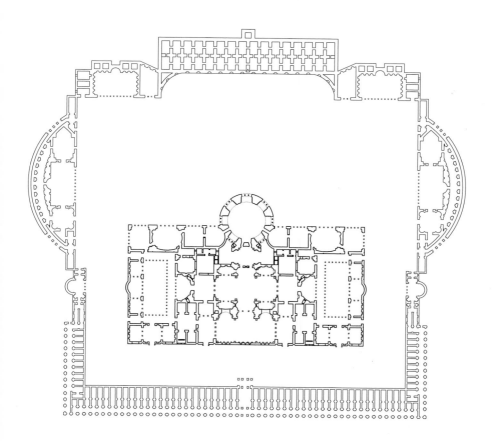

10m

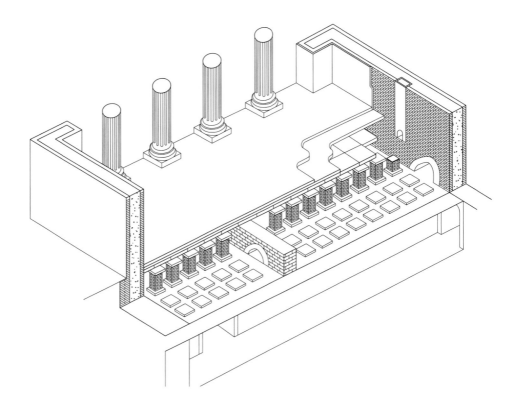

0.5m

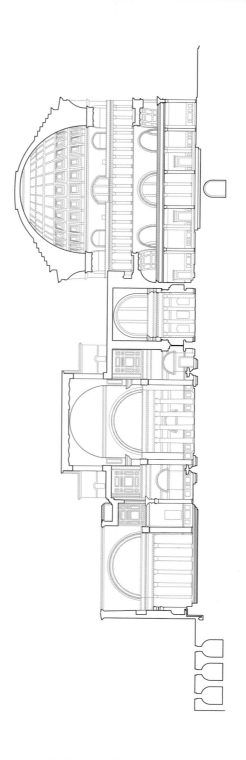

10m

Hagia Sophia
Isidore of Miletus
Anthemius of Tralles

Sean Cullen
Sasha Greig
Kyle Oliver

Initially an Orthodox Christian Church, Hagia Sophia was constructed between 532 - 537. It was converted into a mosque in 1453 and finally into a museum in 1935. Its worn, cracked and undulating floor is made of 6th Century Preconesian book-leaf marble of 600mm in depth. This surface is laid across the expanse of ground, with only slight changes of pattern hinting at the building's various changes in function over time. Slight relief in the floor, demonstrated through level change, signifies the transition from one space to another, most notably between the nave and galleries. As a culturally and religiously significant edifice, entry into the Hagia Sophia through the inner and outer narthex is exaggerated by a number of eşiks. These are threshold stones which are extremely worn and which one must consciously step over, then as a result, enter into the nave with head bowed. Towards the south east of the nave an 'Omphalion', or Coronation Square, is embedded within the marble pavement, adding colour and expression to the vast marble floor.

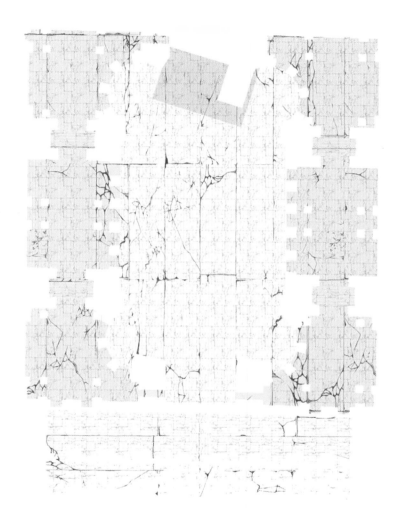

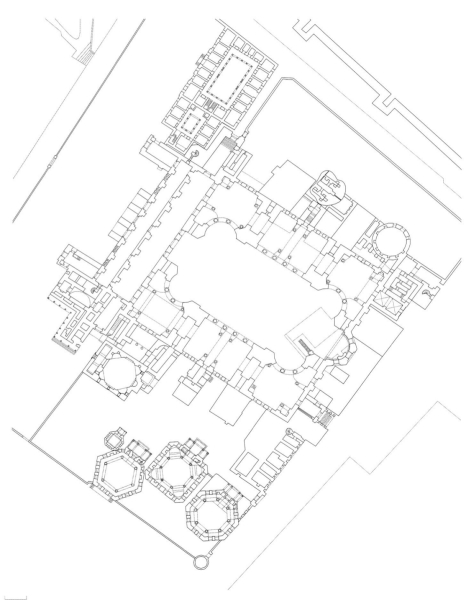

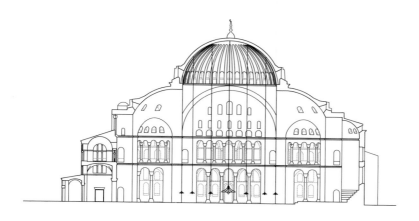

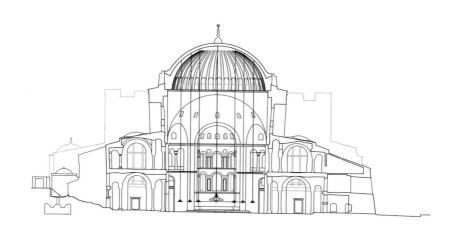

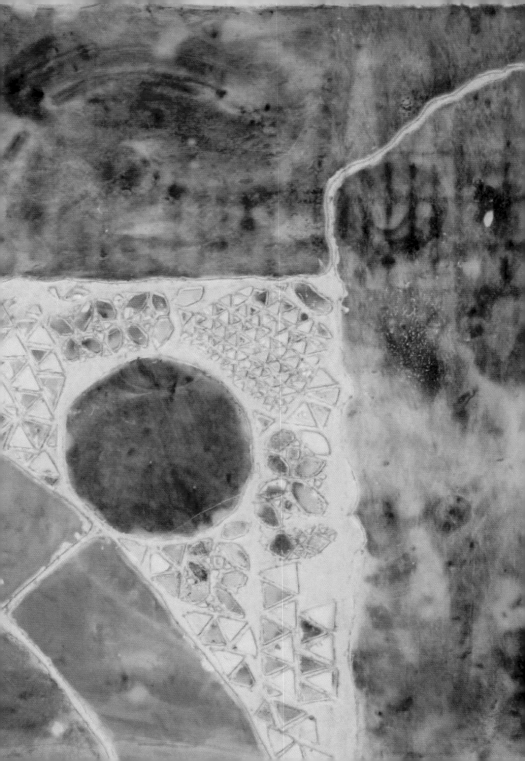

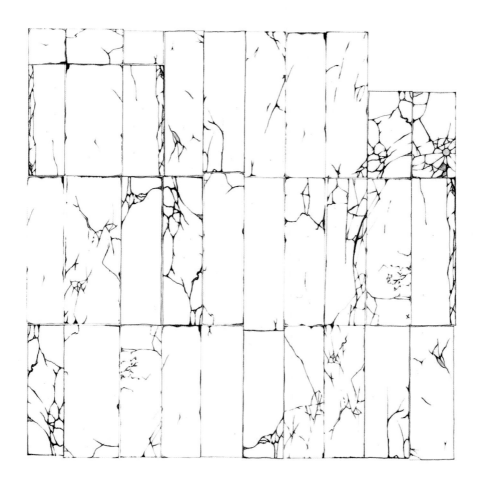

Benedictusberg Abbey, Vaals
Dom Hans van der Laan

Stuart Thompson
Aaron Callen

The Benedictusberg Abbey was founded as a replacement
to the Abbey Merkelbeek in 1897. Over the next century,
several buildings were added to the Abbey, which included the
crypt of Dutch architect and monk, Dom Hans Van Der Laan.
Van Der Laan invented a system of harmonic proportions,
based on studies of human perception of relative scale
called the Plastic Number and left a legacy of architectural
writings arising from his search for fundamental principles
of architecture. In the north-west corner of the abbey
lies the crypt where monks conduct their services. Van
Der Laan used his plastic number as a ratio to structure
the proportions of the crypt. The walls, constructed from
painted brick, lie offset from the concrete grid floor, which
hosts a formation of smooth concrete ground beams and
rough poured concrete in between.

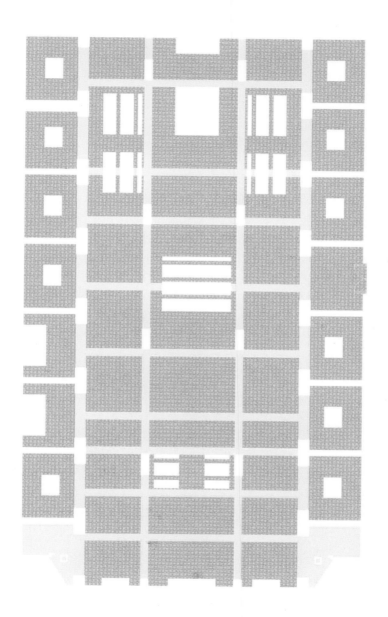

1m

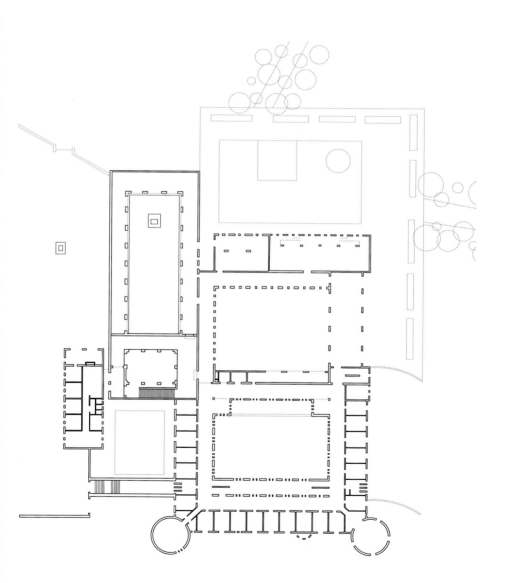

5m

Cloister at Santa Maria della Pace, Italy
Bramante

Rita Farrell
Ciara McCallion

Bramante's Cloister at Santa Maria della Pace was completed in 1503 after the construction of the church in 1482, which was designed by Pontelli. It is likely that Bramante was also responsible for the design of the octagonal dome of the church. The cloister, which comprises of a plan based on a grid of sixteen squares is guided by the laws of proportion and order. The arcade sets up an order and rhythm which suggest a completely orthogonal design. The diagonal geometry at floor level introduces perspective to the scene, which is strengthened by the placement of the entrance at the corner. The square floor slopes gently towards the centre of the cloister, and the intersection between the orthogonal and diagonal axes is marked by a central element, which acts as a drain for water and corresponds in height to the level of the surrounding step. The centre of each side of the cloister is defined by a pier, preventing visual connection with the exterior, and attention is continually drawn back to the introspective centre of the square.

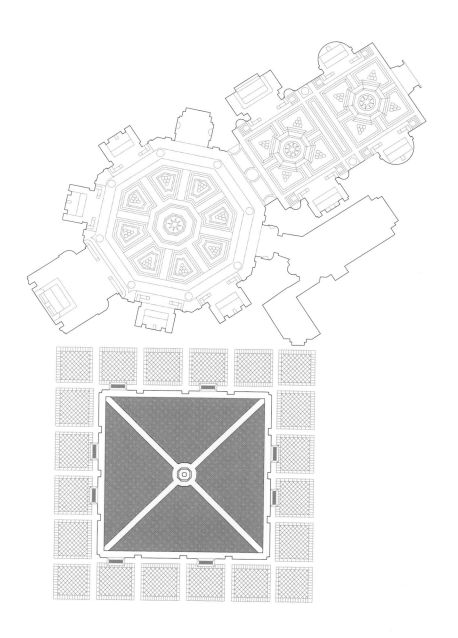

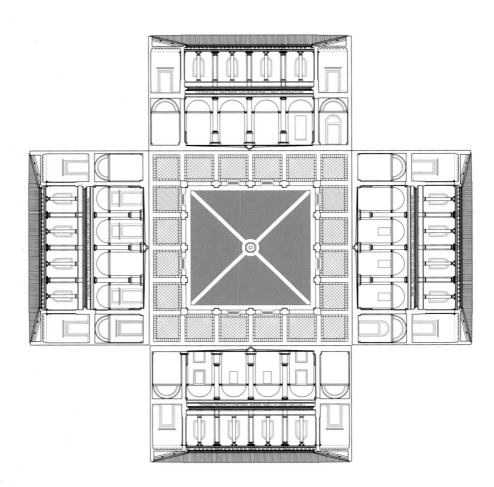

Sinead McGahon
Stephanie Gibbons

Originally designed to support a dome, the octagonal shaped entrance way acts as a central meeting place for Dublin's Regent House. The geometry set up by the space is continued into the symmetrical plan and elevation, and into the hexagonal timber sets of the ground surface. These timber sets, 200mm in depth, were originally employed to dampen the reverberating sound of horse hooves passing through the entrance for the Regent Room above. The hexagonal pattern of the timbers are set into the ground with exposed end grains, providing the surface with a unique tactile character, which has been heavily worn in places from persistent use of this threshold space into Dublin's college campus.

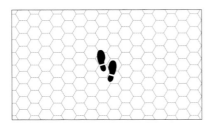

10m

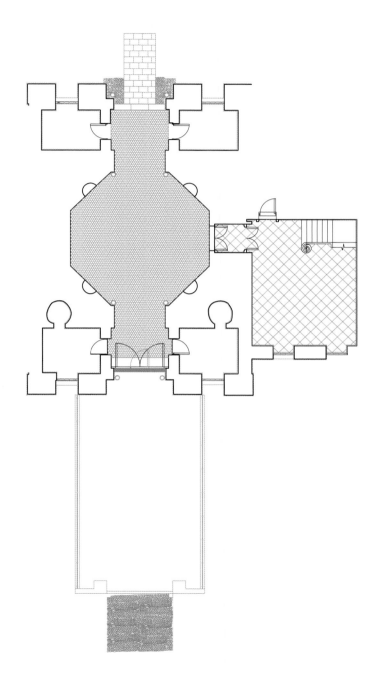

1m

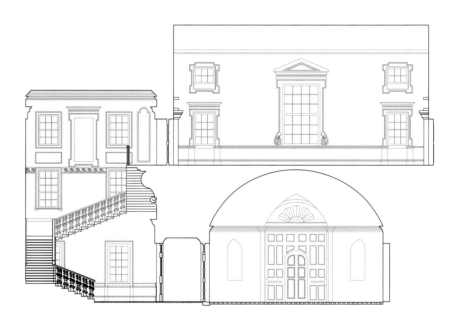

Finbar Bradley
Andrew Hamon
Julian Manev

The foyer of the Philharmonie runs around and underneath the hall linking up all of the various terrace exits of the auditorium at different levels with a profusion of stairs and landings. Partly designed by the sculptor Erich F. Reuther, the floor of the foyer is clad in a mixture of natural stones and mosaics and is said to have been inspired by the work of composer Johannes Sebastian Bach. The laminate nature of the floor is explicitly articulated at the points of rise and drop by the introduction of a vertical white riser tile beneath the projecting blades of the stone treads. The principal axes of the tile grid direct the visitor to the various sets of stairs, ancillary spaces and the neighbouring chamber music hall.

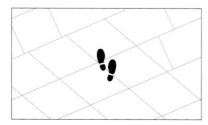

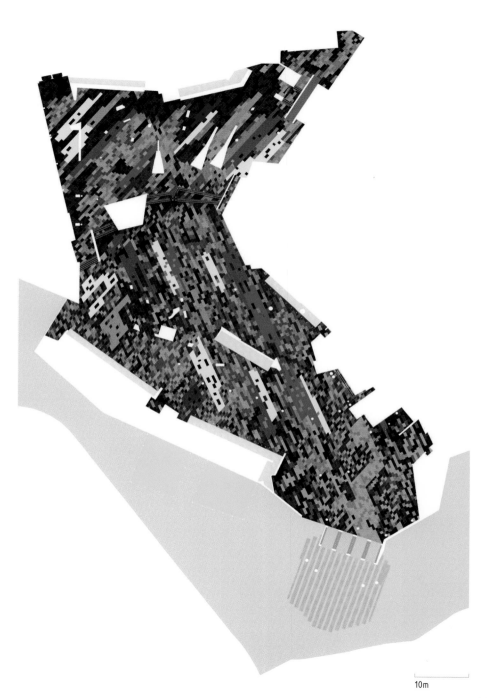

10m

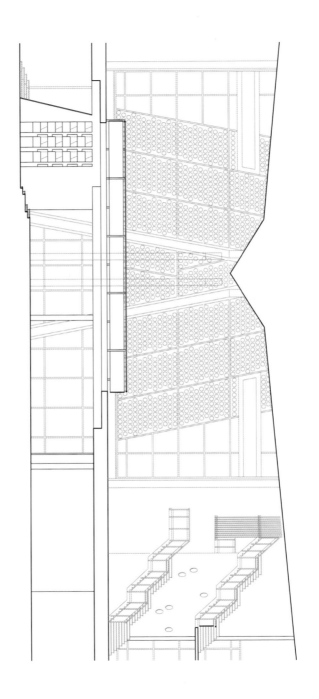

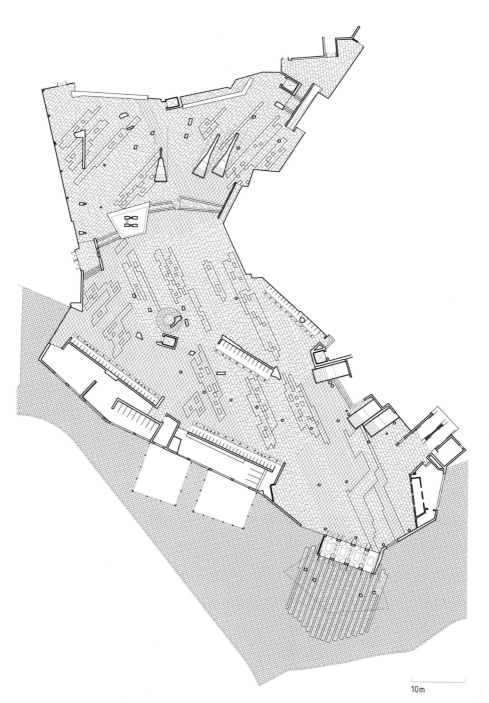

10m

Fondazione Querini Stampalia, Venice
Carlo Scarpa

Mark Kiely
Wouter Lenaerts
Alice Nickell

Carlo Scarpa was commissioned to redesign the interior of the Fondazione Querini Stampalia due to continuous water damage from the connecting canal. Throughout his intervention, Scarpa drew inspiration from the movement and flux of the water levels. His expression of materials, pattern and level changes usher a person from room to room, pattern to pattern, internal to external, and constant to ephemeral. Creating a play of levels - some on which to stop and contemplate, others to move swiftly through - Scarpa manipulates the movement of the spectator's eye across a medley of floor finishes which conduct the rhythm of the journey he has established. A fascinating feature of Scarpa's intervention is a cascade of steps from the canal to a raised and floating walkway. These pull away from the walls, allowing water to flow freely in and under, and create a mini-campo as such. This instance of suspension leads to the feeling of being in between ground level and the canal floor.

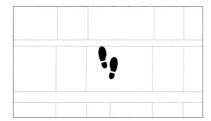

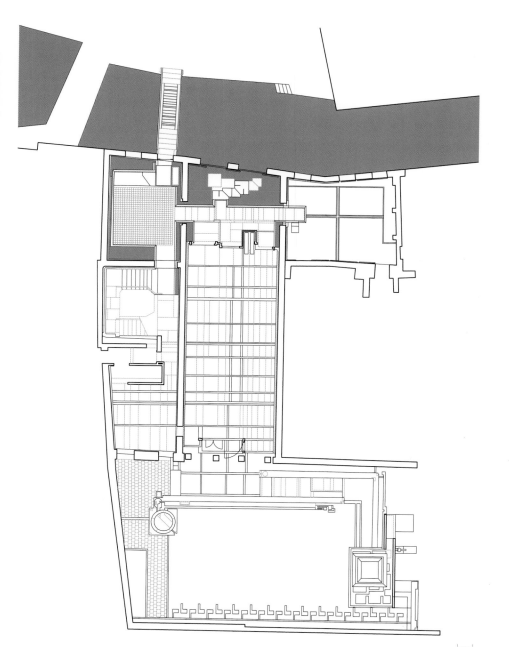

1m

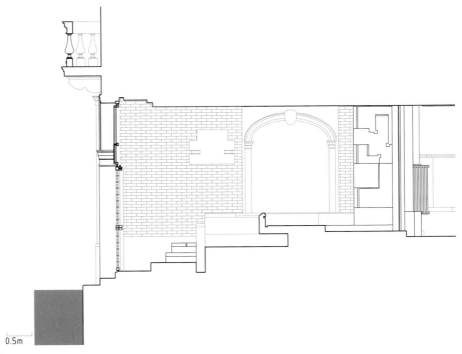

0.5m

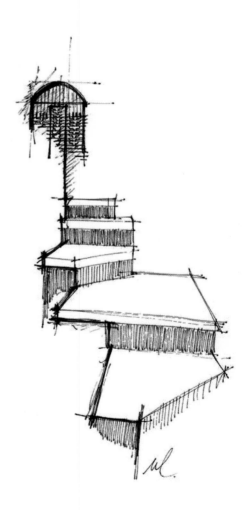

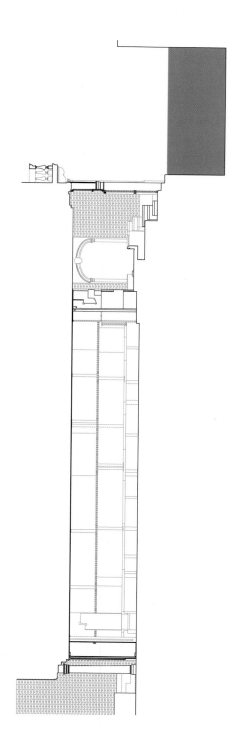

Acropolis Pavement & Church, Athens
Dimitri Pikionis

Justin Hughes
Kaxi Zhang
Megan Nelson-Nilehn

The Acropolis of Athens and its main focal point, the
Parthenon, sit upon a rocky outcrop of the city, and
are accessed via an ascending and formidable path
exposed to the harsh Greek climate. Ascent along
this path is as much a part of the experience as
arrival upon the Parthenon itself. Tasked in the early
1950's with reconfiguring this demanding trail, Greek
architect Demetris Pikionis made careful interventions,
conscious not to detract from either the expedition
or the summit of the journey. Varying compilations
of marble and stone, laid according to vernacular
construction methods, define different phases along
the path. Along steep sections, the path is narrow and
direct with complex stone arrangements, where people
tend to look more at the ground as they strive to
continue along this arduous phase of the route. These
steep sections are also interspersed with benches and
cypress trees for resting and shade, which become less
prominent along gentler sections of the trail and give
way to simpler stone configurations. Pikionis sets up
a clever ambiguity between accidental and purposeful
integration with existing landscape, and heightens the
pedestrian's ritualistic experience along the course of
the Acropolis route.

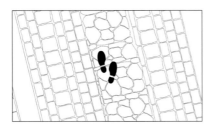

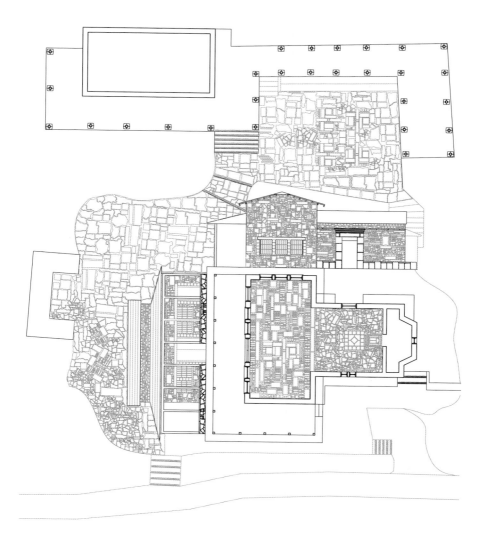

1m

10m

131

Hotel dei Principi, Sorrento, Italy
Gio Ponti

Magdalena Kisiel
Andrew McIlroy

The Hotel de Principi overlooks the Bay of Naples in Sorrento
and is anchored to the rock face which forms an extreme
perimeter to this Mediterranean town. Every aspect of the
blue and white boutique hotel was designed by the architect,
from the building itself to furniture and lighting fixtures.
Ponti worked with local craftsmen to design 30 different
geometric patterned tiles which unfold across the floor
of the hotel. The 30 patterns, comprising of half-moons,
circles and triangles, are laid in a variety of combinations
throughout different spaces and infer a rhythm of patterns
and colours, which are complimented by the blue and white
tones of bespoke fixings. The architect used a uniform floor
tile size throughout, and worked with Italian glazed pottery
known as 'Majolica' tiles. Ponti ensured that each tile was
hand-painted in order to maintain a sense of tactility and
diversity across these large swathes of pattern. The
relentless use of bespoke materials and recurring pattern
combinations bring a curious harmony to the architecture,
most notably the floor which speaks of both craft and luxury.

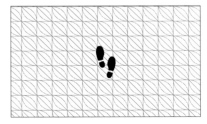

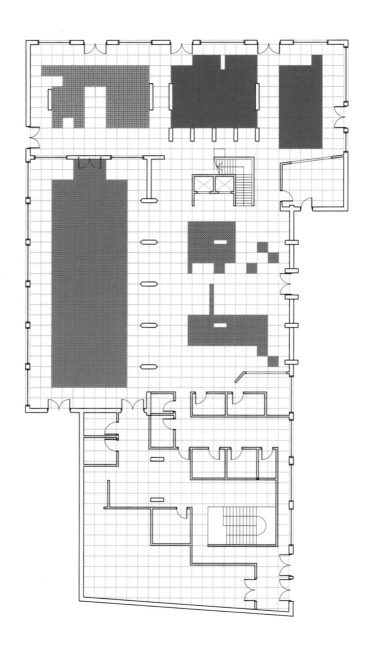

1m

Eixample, Barcelona
Ildefons Cerdà

One of the various zones composing the complex city of
Barcelona in northern Spain is that of the famous Eixample
or 'Expansion' section. The section hosts a floor system laid
onto the city, defining a character by which the urban fabric
is globally recognised. This urban district in the heart of the
city is primarily defined by its rigorous plan which unfurls and
confines the gothic medieval quarter. Designed by Ildefons
Cerdà in the 19th century, the city grid was implemented
in order to alleviate pressure on the gothic quarter at
a time of rapid industrialisation and urban growth. As a
solution, repetitive chamfered blocks and wide boulevards
spread across the ground, carpeting this portion of the city
with a series of airy and bright streets, large octagonal
blocks   and   corresponding   neighbourhood   courtyards.

10m

Manhattan in New York boasts perhaps the world's most
famous city floor. Developed in the 19th century as an
attempt to bring order and balance to the city, the grid was
originally laid out as 2000 blocks with 11 principal avenues
and 155 crosstown streets. The grid, which blankets the
city, initially existed as a completely unbroken and rigorous
plan, hosting 90 degree flat angle blocks to be built upon
and developed. As a testament to the resilience of this
urban grain, the Manhattan grid still flourishes today. Having
adapted to developments in infrastructure, the planar grid
now exists in the vertical dimension also - in the form
of tenements, mass-transit systems and skyscrapers. Now,
where the rigor of the floor framework deviates and the
grid is broken, there occur contrasting profusions of variety
and release from the rigidity of the original city floor.

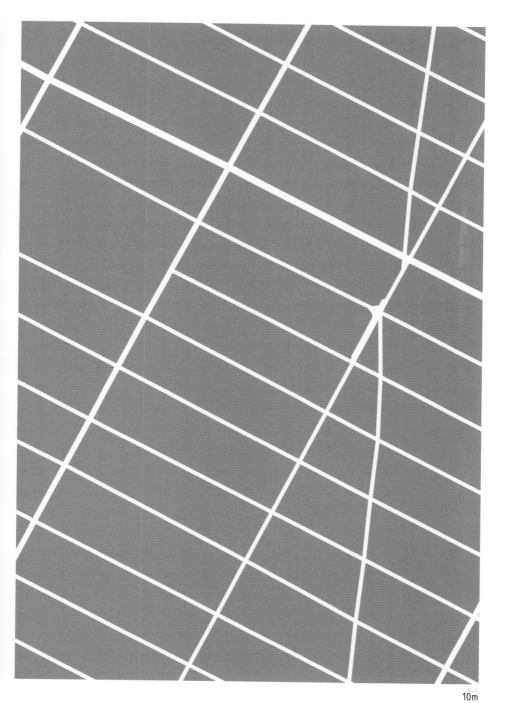

10m

The Radiant City, a title given to Le Corbusier's 1924
vision is an unrealised, yet seminal example of Modernist
utopian ideals. The vision, based on a desire for order and
harmony between humans and their environment, utilised a
totalitarian grid system, constructing an orderly, machine-
like city from the floor upwards. Le Corbusier designed a
linear city, spreading along the ground as uniform plots
for high-rise housing blocks, wide avenues for vehicular
traffic and large areas of green space for leisure and
social activities. The vision for order and efficiency was
to be built, as Le Corbusier imagined, upon the grounds of
demolished vernacular European cities, hence controversially
disregarding the past and looking solely toward the future.
The uniform surfaces spreading across his fictitious urban
centres were stringently symmetrical and unbroken, and in
this regard, again drew criticism for failing to appeal to
the human nature of chance and intuition. Nevertheless,
this judgement of the ground as a means to lay an orderly
city is one which remains influential today, and boasts the
potential to vary in scale- from concentrated application to
a small neighbourhood or to establish a sprawling metropolis.

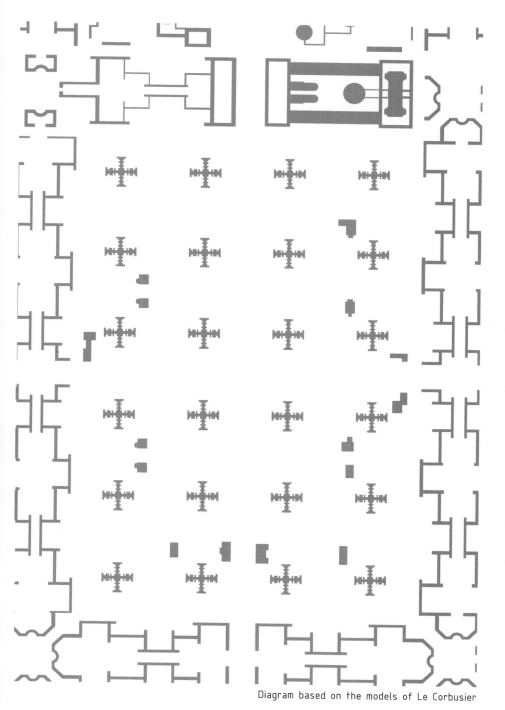

Diagram based on the models of Le Corbusier

Elbows, bends and lyrical space

Michael McGarry

Ridgeway Street sounds like something out of an Ealing comedy – all charm, Englishness and deft touch. This Belfast street is a continuing surprise – a sudden fall from Stranmillis Road in a city that one images as a flat apron laid out under Black Mountain and Divis; houses that have enough in common to establish a loose coherence, but with odd dormers and narrow stepping plots that give a whimsical twist; a line of folded roof planes dropping precariously towards the Lagan, their angles spiking the skyline. The Lyric accounts for the last set of these spiky roofs at the end of the terrace at the bottom of Ridgeway Street.

The entrance is on the footpath – no rhetorical setback or set-down but the immediacy of a domestic front door. Inside there is no letup – ticket office, bench, floor pattern and the edgy pull to rise up the stone stairs towards the light and view. En route the stairs elbow sideways, eroding the box of the overhead rehearsal room; a pause at the top, but the clues continue as the upper foyer folds left and right aligning with the river and wrapping around the theatre. If the access is intense then the upper foyer is relatively calm, a chance to take a breath and compose oneself before the concentration of the theatre space.

Serendipity has much to do with Belfast's character – it is not a set piece but a maze of idiosyncratic occasions and locations. The more bombastic Victorian pieces are well known, but much of Belfast and its charm is this delicate carpet of houses patterned across a subtle landscape. Across this carpet the Lagan winds, generally ignored and yet a singular thread through the city. Its meander and width force an episodic reading of its length; vistas are oblique. The Lyric sits as a fulcrum on one of these leafy bends, an elevated massing seen through the trees, the long diagonal from the high roof point arcing down to the corner of Ridgeway Street. Access from this side is leisurely: grand steps to a terrace then terrace becoming the upper foyer – all quite genteel.

Angled from the foyer through the lobbies into a vessel of a space without a middle aisle, the theatre seems dark and intense. The folded timber side-arches hold the space laterally, the side galleries squeezing like a bellows, the audience and actor confronted. The absence of a central axis maintains the space as indivisible, a scene of anticipation of a shared occasion. For some productions the proscenium arch disappears and audience and actors share the cavern.

The essential strength and value of this architecture is neither its narrative nor its aesthetic but its presence – or, more accurately, its multiple built presences. This building is not a diagram: its complexity and juxtapositions are balanced but never fully reveal themselves in any one move. The entry sequence is one of particularised spaces. The volume over the stairs provides light and scale, but neither simplifies nor centralises; with its brick parapet on one side, timber balustrades on another, and layered and offset circulation, the reading remains complex. The effect is to confront the user with a tectonic reading of the building: brick wall, brick fold, timber screen and concrete soffit confront each other like actors in a drama with the same characters reappearing in different scenes throughout the building. This physicality is at the core of the building's success and is carried right through all moments. No space or

surface is left unconsidered; every element is clearly pronounced like good diction. A meeting room on the third floor has a timber floor and one wall acting together, counterpoised against another wall and ceiling of timber laths, and yet another wall of brick: the room hums, if not buzzes. Relief if needed comes from the views out – to the river, the roofscapes, the street.

The site is difficult, a circumstantial collision of plan geometries on topography like a quarry. The location of the entrance on grade on Ridgeway Street is the key move locking the Lyric to the street and avoiding the obvious exclusive orientation to the river. Planning is exceedingly complex with levels interwoven and a lift magically linking what it must. Other than the central move of passing between the three volumes, the plan is a consequence of the two geometries of Ridgeway Street and the Embankment. But there are multiple other moves: the accordion-like crush of the ground level facade caught between the studio and the rehearsal volumes, the edgy inflections of the stairs, the corporal distortion of the theatre plan, the rotation of the bar foyer pushed by its collision with the upper foyer. The volumetric moves are paralleled in the floor, ceiling, and wall surfaces. Tectonic is the appropriate word for this jostling of volumes in plan and section, stacked like innards.

There are many wonderful moments: the window between the rehearsal room and the upper foyer delivered by the fold and intersection of the two forms, the offset of the main stairs landings, the foyer light fittings and stairs balustrade reaching and stepping like long-limbed creatures, the relationship of upper and bar foyers, the ceiling to the bar foyer, the top floor room looking over roofs to the north and east, the terrazzo boulder of a bar, the picture window to the street from the studio room, the hall bench missing its phone, the modesty onto Ridgeway Street, and the leafy grandeur to the Lagan; the list is long.

The detailing is at the scale of the building: brick as taut skin or lining, concrete as ceiling and shelf, stone as carved, timber as sheet, screen or solid lath. There are no cover slips, no cut bricks, no compromises of assembly; everything conceived in a drawing. The cast concrete copings precisely cap the brick volumes; inside, their roof planes, finished in concrete, are exposed to view. There is nothing ephemeral – all is explicit, directed and resolved like the text of a play. The level of control and the quality of building is extraordinary, much more than the simple out-working of a building contract.

The Lyric opened and lived at the end of its founder Mary O'Malley's back garden – hardly a consequence of design or logic, but one to do with the cocktail of personality and place. Its genesis and its role as a venue for theatre were marvellously matched, with personality, occasion and place counterpoised. It was an inspired and brave choice to remain on the site and not succumb to a diagram of Belfast with its gems hoarded in a notional centre. And so this wonderful and beautifully crafted building – rooted in this place, in Belfast, and this theatre company – is neither generic nor rhetorical but insistent on that same significance of particular place and occasion. Such is architecture, such is theatre.

Michael McGarry is a partner in McGarry Ní Éanaigh Architects, and a Professor of Architecture at Queen's University Belfast
A version of this essay was first published in Perspective, the journal of the Royal Society of Ulster Architects (volume 20, 2011) and subsequently in Architectural Research Quarterly (volume 16, 2012)

Made Ground

Megan Nelson-Nilehn

The Lyric Theatre constructs ground, namely, a platform, from which to look upon the meandering River Lagan. The tight, abruptly sloping site demands a flow between floor levels transforming the hillside into an engaging encounter of people, views and the water below.

The main access is located on the steep fall of Ridgeway Street where the entrance promptly rises to the made ground above. Upon entering, one is pulled towards the light beyond and central void above. An external staircase is placed on the embankment side, where one rises on a stream of concrete steps, like a tributary to the adjacent river. Both accesses are characterised by a steep rise, negotiating existing levels. In spite of this the experience is pleasurable. This is achieved by the continuity and materiality of the stairs as they present an unbroken passage, leaving the storeys less as distinct elements, and more as a continuous and unfurling constructed floor.

The entrance on Ridgeway Street steps immediately off the concrete footpath onto the smooth sandstone floor of the ticket office. This immediate threshold with its proximity to a wall of rising stone steps establishes a draw onto the made ground of the foyer overlooking the river. This harmony of geometries, of rising floor and its fold to wall, compels the gaze to rise. Upon climbing the stone stairs one arrives at an intersection, still sandstone underfoot, a pause where theatre programmes can be purchased. The bar unfolds to the left, with a glazed upper foyer a short flight of sandstone steps to the right. The arrival at the auditorium is announced by a change in ground surface, whereby the brick wall becomes floor. This clay floor defines an area to stop and linger before moving on to watch a performance. This play of sandstone and brick underfoot provides a comfortable, generous sequence of spaces along the route to the auditorium.

From the low, cave-like, emergence and an inclination to look upwards, one is exposed to the concrete soffits and brick walls of the upper levels unfolding above. These concrete soffits appear as shelves, revealing themselves as the underside of floors above rather than simply terminating the space at hand. These moments present the duality of the constructed floor – both an underfoot and overhead experience. Throughout the Lyric the floor becomes a multi-layered component, considered as soffit, boundary, and technical system. The floor assembly is both expressive and seemingly effortless due to the exposure of the concrete slab. The story of how this space is made begins to unfold from the floor.

The Lyric floor is an assemblage of elements. The prosaic build up of differing floor surfaces laid on insulation, under floor heating system on a reinforced concrete slab. These surfaces of brick paving with sand cement joints and coarse buff sandstone pavers construct a new public space in Belfast. Throughout the building sprung timber floors are provided for performance.

The layout of the building creates an open flowing public space – a promenade of path and terrace that meanders and cascades through the building, visually linking internal spaces and offering views out across the river.

Student Design Work

Infrastructure: Belfast Waterworks

Infrastructure can be defined as the non-natural environment which governs the means by which we live: the services that determine how and where things are made and how they are distributed and consumed. One salient characteristic of infrastructures is that they are always composed of networks and systems, of interconnected spaces and technologies that do not exist as autonomous objects but instead are completely interdependent. They are also never static but always somehow in motion, conveying seen or unseen phenomena. Infrastructure is essentially omnipresent and effectively scale-less, ranging from landscape-altering interventions that can be seen from space to the microscopic. This year's M.Arch takes infrastructure as its central theme. It seeks to explore how such systems have developed and continue to develop in Northern Ireland. Infrastructure is never purely a technical concern, instead not only are its effects social but its origins often are too.

The theme of infrastructure was also chosen for its breadth and the many different ways in which it can thought about and responded to architecturally. Accordingly, the M.Arch was divided into four groups each of which have defined a sub-theme, territory or a location. These were representing a wide range of positions from which to consider infrastructure. M.Arch 2013-14 allowed an opportunity to think as architects about a phenomena which is often overlooked, to enquire, understand, critically engage and respond – through architectural space and form – to some of the physical forms, networks and systems that underpin aspects of social life in Northern Ireland. And in doing so, examine the boundaries of architecture.

Our site lies in the Belfast Waterworks located within North Belfast, a key historic domestic foothold and adjacent to one of the city's major arterial roads. The Waterworks is a piece of infrastructure in itself. The land was artificially manipulated to form two large reservoirs. In the 19th century these reservoirs supplied water to the homes of Belfast. The reservoirs became redundant in the mid 20th century and were redeveloped as a recreational center for the ever-increasing population of Belfast. During the troubles, the Waterworks was integrated into the social engineering of the city peace lines. Essentially acting as a buffer zone between nationalist and protestant communities.

The site presents opportunities for integration both in the physical form, but also in the social reaction of the surrounding community and the city of Belfast. The relationship of the life of the building into the life of the city was a core matter to investigate as part of the project.

Photograph page 151 : Michelle Reuter

"The year long working drawing programme for the Second Arts Building at Bath necessitated the forming of rules, not only to maintain the consistency and quietness of detail but to establish an investigation tool for understanding the spaces of the building. Strategic plans at a scale of 1:200 were the first drawings, closely followed by detail fragments of the building drawn at 1:25 scale and full size. Probably the last drawings to be made were the 1:100 assembly plans. There was a constant trawling for information, back and forth between strategy and detail. In the beginning the invention of precise detail in relation to strategy was a necessity for understanding the building, gradually, over the course of the working drawing period, these rule systems were used to temper invention and verify intuition."

Peter Salter, Climate Register,
Four works by Alison & Peter Smithson, AA

This semester we intended to explore the way people move through, experience and inhabit interior space. Our brief was to accommodate a home for the Belfast School of Contemporary Dance. Our site is on the embankment of the Belfast water works. We were invited to consider the project infra-structurally both in its siting on lands resultant from infrastructure, but also in how the technologies of the floor can act to enable a rich diversity of activities both internal and external to the major functions of the brief.

The mission of the Belfast School of Dance is to provide an environment conducive to the highest caliber of dance training, art making and scholarship. The school will promote fluidity between the processes of making art, honing craft and deepening intellectual explorations. The core brief for the building was to provide spaces which nurture exceptional dance practitioners, allows them to make creative and intellectual contributions to the larger dance community, and fosters collaborative endeavours within and beyond the field.

Gareth Taylor

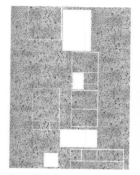

Ciara McCallion

PC Wan

Michael McKeown

James Boyd

James Grieve

Jill Richardson

Aine Grace

Aaron Callen

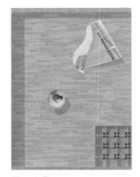

Stuart Thompson

Conor Kerr

Eva McGowan

Julian Manev

Ronnie Murray

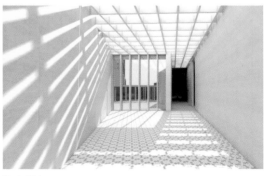

Mark Kiely

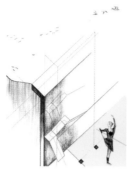

Antonis Stylianou

Alice Nickell

Megan Nelson-Nilehn

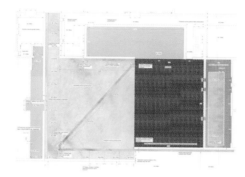

Nadine Graham

Orla McCann

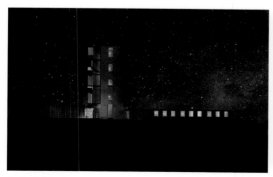

Andrew Hamon

James McCallister

Cormac McAteer

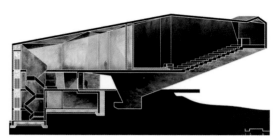

Declan Price

Naomi Sheehan

Tom Cosgrove

Finbar Bradley

Jason Stead

Sinead McGahon

Fergal Rainey   Andrew Abraham   Sean Sloan

Aoife McConaghy   Patrick Hoban   Ryan O'Neill

Kyle Oliver

Undulating Ground

Shelley McNamara
Grafton Architects

When we visited Milan during the course of the Bocconi University Competition, we were struck by the potency of the stone floor of the city, particularly since Viale Bligny, where our site was located, was paved in this typical thick pink granite. Sadly this stone paving has now been replaced by tarmacadam on Viale Bligny but still exists in many Milanese streets.

We wanted to bring the life of the city into the university and to bring with it the stone floor of the city. This thinking about the stone floor was one of the key starting points for the project. When we had made this decision we then started to think about the ground as a new 'platform', a new piece of urban landscape. Because of Utzon's writings about platforms in architecture, Mayan architecture for example, we were looking at the new platform which he constructed for the Sydney Opera House. We were struck by the fact that he was constructing a 'new geology' a new island, from which the building would grow.

We then thought about the Bocconi project as a new undulating ground, an urban landscape, erupting and cut, to form the spaces at ground level and below. There was a previous planning permission for the Bocconi site, with an established height restriction, so the brief was to bury half the accommodation below ground. This working of the ground allowed us to bring light into the sunken spaces, and we thought about the aula manga as a solid stone element rising out of the stone floor.

When we had formed this idea of a stone platform, it raised the question as to how we would 'place' elements on top of it. We wanted to preserve as much of the stone platform as possible, so as to allow the life of the city into the building. Three elements were freely placed on this new ground. The foyer to the sunken aula manga and conference rooms, the entrance hall for the 1000 professors who were to occupy the research offices above, and the cafe.

The large 25m span of the primary structure was chosen since we were trying to make a 'piece of city', an urban infrastructure, a building at the scale of the city. Preserving the openness of stone floor of the city, led us to the decision to suspend this smaller scale labyrinth of offices from large roof beams supported by the large scale primary structure. This suspended research world hovers over the floor of the city, with voids and courts allowing light to enter deep into the ground and basement levels.

The experience of making the Bocconi University Building, together with working on more recent projects such as the Toulouse School of Economics at University UT1 Capitol, and the UTEC University of Engineering in Lima, has led us to develop the idea that each new project we make is a piece of new ground, a new geology, a new geography.

Through this body of work, and this scale of work, we have reflected on what is happening to the world around us. As more and more of the natural world disappears, as more and more people now live in cities, we are reassessing the role of the new urban 'places' and environments we are making. We believe that these environments need to actively reinstate the balance between man and nature, need to connect people with the time of day, with the seasons, with landscape, with bird life, with the sky, with the ground.

How we as architects make floors and platforms is part of this reassessment. A sloping floor where we feel the contours of the ground, an excavated floor where we feel the 'cut' in the ground, a suspended floor where we feel that we are floating over real ground, a floor that efficiently and beautifully drains the rainwater, a floor that is in shade and is cold, a floor that is in the sunshine and is warm, a floor that becomes a staircase, a bridge, a seat. These are architectural decisions with which we continually grapple, to find the beginnings of a project or to find the end result.

The floor is the surface that 'grounds' us, anchors us, centers us as human beings on this earth. We should feel the earth's surface below us, if it is rock, stable, hard, or if it is soft, pliable, unstable like peat or sand.

Fernando Tavora speaks beautifully about gravity, "when we use the word we evoke both the notion of weight and of intelligent and thoughtful action. Let us not forget that gravity, physical or plastic contributes to the temporal or symbolic stability of architecture". Constructing the floor relates to this "temporal or symbolic gravity".

Shelley McNamara is a Director of Grafton Architects. The Universita Luigi Bocconi, School of Economics in Milan was the recipient of the World Building of the Year Award 2008, the Learning Category Award at the World Architecture Festival 2008 and the Downes Medal of the Architectural Association of Ireland.

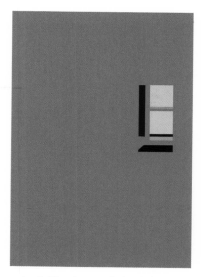

www.queensarchitecuralpress.com